MANAGING STAGE FRIGHT

MANAGING STAGE FLIGHT

MANAGING
STAGE FRIGHT

*A Guide for Musicians
and Music Teachers*

JULIE JAFFEE NAGEL

OXFORD
UNIVERSITY PRESS

OXFORD
UNIVERSITY PRESS

Oxford University Press is a department of the University of Oxford. It furthers
the University's objective of excellence in research, scholarship, and education
by publishing worldwide. Oxford is a registered trade mark of Oxford University
Press in the UK and certain other countries.

Published in the United States of America by Oxford University Press
198 Madison Avenue, New York, NY 10016, United States of America.

© Oxford University Press 2017

Library of Congress Cataloging-in-Publication Data
Names: Nagel, Julie Jaffee.
Title: Managing stage fright : a guide for musicians and music teachers /
Julie Jaffee Nagel.
Description: New York, NY : Oxford University Press, [2017] |
Includes bibliographical references and index.
Identifiers: LCCN 2017003887| ISBN 9780190632038 (pbk. : alk. paper) |
ISBN 9780190632021 (hardcover : alk. paper)
Subjects: LCSH: Music—Performance—Psychological aspects. |
Performance anxiety.
Classification: LCC ML3830 .N333 2017 |
DDC 781.4/3111—dc23
LC record available at https://lccn.loc.gov/2017003887

9 8 7 6 5 4 3 2
Paperback printed by WebCom, Inc., Canada
Hardback printed by Bridgeport National Bindery, Inc., United States of America

With gratitude to
my music and my psychoanalytic teachers,

my patients,
and my former piano students

CONTENTS

LIST OF ILLUSTRATIONS

Figures

Charts

Tables

PREFACE

EVERY STUDENT AND PERFORMER PROBABLY has been asked, "How long do you practice every day?" A similar question, "How long did it take you to write this book?" is posed to book authors. In responding to the latter query, I can say that it has taken this author a lifetime to write this book on stage fright. As a performing pianist, I experienced stage fright, and as a psychotherapist and psychoanalyst, I have treated and made presentations to numerous others who experience stage fright. My thinking about this imposing topic is lifelong and remains a work in progress.

In one respect, this book is somewhat autobiographical. In writing about stage fright, I have tapped into my winding journey from being trained as a classically trained musician at Juilliard and my second education at the University of Michigan in psychology and social work. Subsequently, I was trained as a psychoanalyst at the Michigan Psychoanalytic Institute. During past years, I have worked as an independent piano teacher, performer, and teacher of general music in public schools. For over 30 years post-Juilliard and the

University of Michigan graduations, I have been a psycho-therapist, psychoanalyst, author, and presenter. I have always held the conviction that mental health is an integral part of a music education and the teacher–student relationship. I have been fascinated with stage fright and its effects on mental health, and I have studied it from multiple perspectives.

The common thread in my personal and professional journey has been my interest in relationships with people, and my curiosity about what makes them "tick." In this book, I share my experiences, research and clinical findings from my hybrid education, and lessons I have learned from my former piano students and patients. In doing so, I elaborate on my own travels, travails, and discoveries about performance anxiety. I have found the journey energizing, rigorous, at times difficult, full of unexpected discoveries about myself and others, and yet always vibrant and satisfying. My personal journey will be ongoing after this book is completed. I hope your journey will continue after you finish reading the last chapter. The topic of stage fright is eternally fascinating.

The purpose of this book is to offer independent and college music teachers, music students, and music performers psychological information and practical guidelines about the psychology and management of performance anxiety. The information in this book is also relevant for piano pedagogy and music education courses. Parents of music students also could benefit from understanding the power of stage fright experienced by their children and acquire some management techniques for helping them. Further, many people besides musicians struggle with performance anxiety. These include speakers, academics, writers, people in the arts, athletes, and those individuals with social anxieties.

In order to accomplish the goal of better understanding stage fright, the focus is on the centrality of the music teacher in students' musical and emotional development. Even for those performers or students who are not currently studying with teachers, the imprint of the music teacher is embedded forever inside one's mind. It is not unusual for performers to "hear" the teacher's advice and feel the teacher's presence from lessons that may have occurred long ago. Internalized mentally by current and former students, the music teacher accompanies performers of all ages inside their minds every time they appear in public.

The uniqueness of the music teacher–music student relationship is the prism through which this book unfolds, as some of the mysteries of stage fright are unraveled, and strategies are offered for understanding its unwelcome presence and uncomfortable consequences. The music studio and what occurs in the teacher–student relationship provide the ideal situation for understanding performance anxiety. The information is generalizable to other performers who are not involved in music performance.

Every chapter is organized around helping teachers become tuned in to subtle (and sometimes puzzling) symptoms and behaviors that are part of a larger and deeper panorama of students' emotional health. While examining stage fright from multiple psychological perspectives, practical strategies are offered that will inform and empower teachers to inform and empower students. While this is not a "how to" book that offers specific advice, it is a book that encourages deeper understanding of oneself, and the encouragement to make use of multiple options that are presented that can be helpful in reducing stage fright. The leitmotif throughout the chapters that follow emphasizes that music lessons are life lessons.

Several theoretical, clinical, and practical frameworks are offered, since no single approach has a monopoly on the complex topic of stage fright or how to work with students' individual needs. A single psychological theory (or musical/pedagogical approach) does not fit all people. Teachers and students are too complex to be reduced to a formula.

A recurring theme throughout the book is explained through an A B C model that is applicable to various psychological theories. Teachers can assist students (and themselves) to recognize and understand feelings, thoughts, and physical reactions to anxiety—all represented symbolically by Letter B.

Thus, teachers are encouraged both to (1) understand the complex dynamics of stage fright (represented by Letter B) and (2) offer concrete strategies that are offered throughout the book to help lower student anxiety (also represented by Letter B). The reader will realize that Letter B represents a theoretical and practical metaphor and organizing model, regardless of theoretical orientation.

While the psychology of stage fright is presented from psychodynamic, behavioral, and developmental psychological perspectives, the overarching theme emphasizes lifelong human development. Understanding the music student as a whole person (i.e., a person who brings a life history, a biological predisposition, a social background, and a personal narrative to each lesson and every performance) enhances teaching, learning, and performing.

Music teachers are integral to students' psychological and musical development. An argument with a parent or friend, being bullied at school, the loss of a favorite pet, a disappointing grade on a test, an illness, a friend moving out of town, a divorce in the family, and numerous other life events can interfere with the student's learning and pleasure in making music. Such occurrences compromise a student's ability to concentrate on work and can lower self-confidence. One teacher commented, "Students never arrive at lessons with a clean emotional slate for learning." I agree with this observation.

It is not unusual for any teacher to be the first responder to students who may or may not talk about their concerns. This is particularly salient for music teachers who come into contact with students on a one-to-one basis or in a special group or group situation such as instrumental, vocal music, music theory, and history. Often, emotional distress will be evident through a student's performance, attendance, and attitude, particularly in the guise of chronic, often debilitating, performance anxiety and expressions of self-doubt. Teachers often will detect subtle clues that "something doesn't feel right." Most music teachers have the best of intentions and exquisite empathy, but they are not trained professionally to deal with benign, festering, or acute emotional problems.

The chapters are organized around a format that raises questions, discusses theoretical and practical responses, and offers activities and teaching strategies that can be used in the studio or class. Each chapter concludes with a summary of points relevant to the material offered. Performance anxiety is explored from several psychological lenses intended to offer multiple ways to conceptualize and use information regarding thoughts, emotions, and actions (Letter B) that are expressed in the teaching studio.

Performance anxiety is discussed with the goal of management rather than elimination, since anxiety cannot be eliminated, but it can be transformed into creative energy once better understood. It is possible and desirable for teachers to assist students in developing skills and attitudes so students will not feel overwhelmed by strong feelings. Students and teachers can use psychological concepts both in music lessons and in a variety of life situations.

Readers will also be introduced to psychological principles that address the formation of anxiety and how various thought processes create psychological defenses to ward off anxiety when threats to integrity and competence are perceived. Performance anxiety is extraordinarily complex, and stage fright begins long before the student walks into the teaching studio or on stage. I propose that stage fright actually begins in the nursery. A lifelong developmental perspective on performance anxiety provides a broad context for understanding students.

A novel approach to pulling the all the chapters together in a practical way for teachers is offered by way of a synthesis called "A Virtual Recital." An imaginary teacher coaches an imaginary student through a recital (away from the instrument) using concepts from all of the psychological frameworks with emphasis on thoughts, feelings, and behaviors represented by Letter B, which have been offered in earlier chapters.

Each chapter concludes with "implications for teachers" as a way to organize the material. The final chapters offer additional suggestions for thinking about stage fright, including the relevance of using this book in music education courses, pedagogy classes, and discussion groups as well as in private studios, studio classes, and even at home. The book offers a glossary of technical terms to reiterate important ideas and provide concise definitions of concepts.

Numerous illustrative readings on stage fright are provided should the teacher wish to pursue this important topic further. It should be noted that most of these extant references are directed toward performers rather than teachers, making this book an original resource for teachers. The information provided will add psychological strategies to teacher's pedagogy toolboxes.

All people take a unique life history, begun in the nursery, into lessons, classes, on stage when performing, and off stage when the final note has sounded. A personal history sits beside and resides inside the mind of every performer and teacher. The impact of our emotional lives impacts everything we do, including teaching, making music, and dealing with stage fright. Clearly, students and teachers are greater than the sum of their musical parts.

It is my sincere hope that teachers will find this book informative, useful, creative, reassuring, and thought provoking. As teachers learn to significantly help students understand and handle stage fright and integrate this knowledge into their teaching and their self-reflections about themselves, my objectives in blending psychological concepts, informed attitudes, and teaching strategies will be accomplished.

ACKNOWLEDGMENTS

ONE CANNOT MAKE THE ARDUOUS journey alone toward understanding stage fright. I appreciate the people who have encouraged me, taught me, and influenced my direction at every stage to better understand my own performance anxiety. When I began the doctoral program in psychology and social work at the University of Michigan, many years after I completed two degrees at Juilliard, my advisor told me that I would change in unforeseen ways. During a conference, after my first year of study, she commented, "I knew you would change, but I had no idea it would be this much and this soon." I am deeply grateful to all of my teachers, mentors, and colleagues who provided the impetus to explore uncharted places in my mind that I never could have imagined. They all encouraged me to think creatively and deeply. I was wisely advised not to accept the first thought that came into my mind as the last word on any subject.

I am grateful for the support from extraordinary psychoanalytic teachers, mentors, and colleagues from both the American Psychoanalytic Association and the Michigan Psychoanalytic Institute. Special individuals include the late Stuart Feder and the late Pinchas Noy. Glen Gabbard, Channing Lipson, Roy Schafer, Melvin Lansky, Salman Akhtar, Stefan Pasternack, Curtis Bristol, and Charles Burch continue to enrich my thinking. My psychoanalyst, Peter Blos Jr., encouraged me to discover anchors within myself when the headwinds (literally and figuratively) were strong and formidable.

Steven Paledes, my high school piano teacher; Jerry Lowder, my high school choir director (for whom I was the accompanist for the Newport News High School Chorus), and Josef Raieff, my piano teacher at Juilliard, had profound influences on me. My professor and advisor at the University of Michigan, Jesse Gordon, whom I met many years ago when I returned to graduate school at the University of Michigan, is the inspiration for the "virtual recital" chapter at the end of this book. This "recital" made its debut in his research class, has been revised for this book, and is dedicated to him. The late Edward Bordin, the cochair of my dissertation committee (with Jesse Gordon) broadened my understanding of the importance of career as it is connected to one's personality and self-image.

My colleagues at the Music Teachers National Association who have endorsed and invited my contributions on music teaching and mental health include Gail Berenson, Gary Ingle, and Brian Shepard. Their support of my presentations that consider the student as a "whole person" were cosponsored by the American Psychoanalytic Association and led to a significant collaboration at the 2016 MTNA National Conference in San Antonio, Texas, the 2017 MTNA National

Conference in Baltimore, Maryland, and future interdisciplinary outreach between two highly respected national organizations. I look forward to deepening this ongoing relationship. I am grateful to Dean Stein, executive director, and Carolyn Gatto, scientific programs and meeting director, at the American Psychoanalytic Association for their support of my work and for facilitating funding from the American Psychoanalytic Foundation to present at the MTNA Conference in Las Vegas in 2015. These individuals and the recognition from the Michigan Psychoanalytic Institute, where I was trained in psychoanalysis, have contributed to my interdisciplinary curiosity, scholarship, and clinical skills. I also have enjoyed my association with the Frances Clark Center for Keyboard Pedagogy. Peter Jutras, editor-in-chief of *Clavier Companion*, graciously invited me to be a contributing editor through my regular column, "Mind Matters." His editorial comments are always sensitive and insightful.

E. L. Lancaster, vice president and keyboard editor-in-chief at Alfred Music Company was supportive and encouraging in getting this book launched. His professionalism, integrity, and dedication to musicians' mental health are extraordinary and deeply appreciated.

Suzanne Ryan, Executive Editor of Music and Editor-in-Chief of Humanities at Oxford University Press, offered encouragement and invaluable insights about writing this book from our first communication. Her enthusiasm, encouragement, and editorial expertise are reflected on every page. Eden Piacitelli, former editorial assistant at Oxford University Press, and Victoria Kouznetsov, and Celine Aenlle-Rocha, have been helpful in guiding my project from proposal to completed book. Samara Stob, assistant marketing manager, has enabled this book to reach a broad readership. Jayme Johnson has promoted my work and generously shared wise and practical ideas with me. My thanks are extended also to the anonymous editors and reviewers who made comments on early drafts of my manuscript. Their keen observations have assisted my attempts to make complex concepts come alive more clearly.

I have always been inspired and motivated by my former piano students and current and past psychotherapy and psychoanalytic patients, who have the courage to think deeply about their stage fright and who have trusted me in our work together. I have learned a great deal from them.

My daughter, Sonya Lewis, has created many significant melodies in my life with her passion for music, her training in medicine, and her exquisite sensitivity for others. David Lewis, my son-in-law, has been a valuable resource personally and professionally in providing camera-ready charts and tables for this book. His portfolio as an architect now includes drawings to illuminate performance anxiety. My granddaughters, Sarah and Rachel, provide more joyful and vibrant counterpoint in my life than I can communicate here.

My late mother, Elizabeth Lichtenstein Jaffee, and my grandparents, Julian and Esther Lichtenstein, knew I was intent on becoming a concert pianist since I was a very young child. They bought an upright piano for me when I was five years old and purchased my first baby grand piano when I was eleven years old. They unswervingly supported my decision to pursue music as my life's work. Sadly, none of them lived long enough to share my satisfaction in also becoming a psychoanalyst and subsequently combining my music and psychology/psychoanalytic educations. They were the most loving audience anyone could ever want.

My hybrid musical and psychological journey could not have been launched or sustained without the support of my husband, Louis. His enormous musical and pianistic gifts and encouragement have been inspiring since we first met at Juilliard.

MANAGING STAGE FRIGHT

MANAGING STAGE FRIGHT

STAGE FRIGHT

What Is It?

QUESTIONS FOR THOUGHT

- What is stage fright?
- What causes it?
- How can students and teachers understand it?
- How can performers handle it?
- How can teachers help students manage it?

SOME GENERAL CONSIDERATIONS ABOUT STAGE FRIGHT

Stage fright is a formidable challenge for musicians of all ages and levels of accomplishment. Perhaps the phrase "performance anxiety" is a more correct term because no one is frightened literally by a stage. Many performing musicians experience anxiety when they go onto a stage. "Performance anxiety" and "stage fright" are two phrases that are used interchangeably in this volume. With psychological and physical symptoms such as shaking, memory slips, insecurity despite excellent preparation, fear of ridicule by an audience that leads to embarrassment and shame, and the worry that "something must be wrong with me," stage fright has the potential to undermine the best-prepared performer. Stage fright diabolically threatens self-confidence and self-esteem. Therein lie both the problem and an opportunity for an emphasis on important coping strategies. This book will help teachers understand the problems and symptoms of stage fright in their students and offer coping strategies to enhance students' self-esteem.

Performance anxiety can be mystifying. While it comes alive on stage, performance anxiety does not begin on stage, nor is it the private domain of musicians. Stage fright is ubiquitous. For example, some students may chronically under-perform in exams or are so anxious that studying becomes impossible. Additionally, there is high performance anxiety about acing MCATS, LSATS, and other gate-keeping exams for admission to graduate schools. Anxiety about job interviews and career decisions doggedly plague talented and competent people. Some physicians, psychologists, and other professionals find careers and egos are threatened due to not being able to stand before peers and present their research at conferences.

It is not uncommon for university students, in their final year of study, suddenly to become test phobic and anxious about careers post graduation. Athletes face clutch situations routinely where all eyes are on them to make a basket, a touchdown, a goal, or a home run. Many ambitious CEOs and business executives cannot present reports at meetings without self-doubt and fear that they will appear incoherent and incompetent. It is not a long distance emotionally from the boardroom to the bedroom, where couples often struggle with intimacy around performance anxiety.

Clearly, for musicians and many others, performance anxiety brews unconsciously and develops silently as life experiences, thoughts, physical sensations, affects in performers' minds, and feelings in the body long before it announces its unwelcome presence on stage. Stage fright has a long incubation period. Performance anxiety begins in childhood. This is particularly pertinent for understanding musicians.

One logically asks, can this mental menace be tamed? Performance anxiety can be better understood, and, with understanding, this diabolical threat can become facilitating rather than debilitating. Music teachers can assist students of all ages and levels of ability in this endeavor.

A PERSONAL REFLECTION

Allow me to share an autobiographical note. I have known performance anxiety almost my entire life. My first acquaintance with stage fright occurred when I was about six years old. I recently had begun piano lessons and was also composing short compositions. My piano teacher decided to audiotape some of my compositions. I will never forget how, in the middle of the recording session, I had a memory slip—my first. I could not remember my own music. I still remember whispering in panic, "Stop the record, stop the record!!!"

I recall to this day the feelings of humiliation and shame that my mistake would be permanently documented. (Yes, six-year-olds experience humiliation and embarrassment and shame and other strong feelings that should not be dismissed as "childish.") I still remember that awful anxiety, feeling confused, and not understanding what was happening. It was *my* music that *I* had composed. *How could I forget my own music?* It was impossible for me at the age of six to understand what was occurring or have the control to stop my panic or halt the recording. I believed that my memory slip would be permanently recorded. It would be documented forever.

I wish that my teacher had understood my emotional distress and turned off the tape recorder. I wish that she had assisted me. But we continued to record. This traumatic experience is etched forever in my mind. It has powerfully informed my thinking, my education in piano performance, my career change to psychology and psychoanalysis, my research, my clinical orientation, my public presentations, and my writing. I call this audiotape my "forever recording."

Younger and older students experience performance anxiety just as I did. Teachers can be the gateway to recognizing distress and helping them. There are strategies to understand performance anxiety that are useful for teachers to employ in assisting anxious students of any age and any stage of musical and psychological development. That assistance is what this book has to offer.

MUSIC TEACHERS AS MENTAL HEALTH RESOURCES

In addition to teaching music, music teachers are mental health resources. The "answers" for performance anxiety do *not* lie in "practicing harder—or longer." (Yes, students must practice diligently and intelligently. There is no substitute for quality preparation.) Students cannot "talk themselves out" of performance anxiety by following some protocol that is prescribed by an "expert" with fancy credentials. Many students believe that they are the *only* person with performance anxiety, and they harbor uncomfortable feelings silently. Teachers should speak openly about stage fright with students. This communication should be a "norm" in the studio and classroom. Teachers can learn to become more aware of the psychological messages students convey and offer tools to assist them.

Like a fugue, performance anxiety has many contrapuntal layers; like a musical composition, it has many themes—originating overtly and dramatically and/or subtly and quietly in the exposition of childhood. Layers of life development evolve into a highly complex tapestry of emotions and beliefs about oneself. Performance puts one's self-esteem as well as talent on the line in public.

After parents and close family, teachers are often the most important people in a young student's life. Music teachers, particularly private instrumental teachers who work with students on a one-to-one basis over a period of years, have relationships with students that are rare among the general teaching (or any other) profession. They are frequently "first responders." This is an enormous honor, a huge responsibility, and an important challenge.

What happens to the joy in making music when a student feels anxious about playing in a recital? For many students, a recital introduces fears and self-doubts, embarrassment about making mistakes, humiliation and fear about memory slips, worries about pleasing others, being rejected or scorned, and sometimes, outright panic and terror. In one way, it seems paradoxical that stage fright develops at all given that a student practices regularly and intelligently, is taught carefully by an expert teacher, and is smart and industrious. Stage fright is a bully!

PARADOXICAL QUESTIONS AND FURTHER THOUGHTS ABOUT STAGE FRIGHT

* Why does nervousness, experienced physically with shaking and psychologically with self-doubt, roar like an angry lion and interfere with a sense of competence in a performance that could be a pleasurable experience?
* Why do students have trouble reassuring themselves that they are fully prepared, and that preparation is a great "insurance policy" for performing well on stage?
* If the playing goes "perfectly" (or well enough) in the practice room, why does not the same thing happen on stage?
* How can music teachers help students learn to cope effectively with a lack of confidence and anxieties that surface in public?

It would not be helpful to totally "get rid" of performance anxiety. Using a cooking analogy, the right amount of spice enhances the recipe. If there is too little spice, the food is not tasty. If there is too much spice, it overpowers the food. The same metaphor applies to electricity—just enough electricity can heat a home or cook food. Too much electricity causes a house to go up in flames or burn dinner. Mental energy in the mind works that way with anxiety and stage fright.

Performers need to have, or develop, the "right," or optimum, amount of mental energy to add spice to a performance.

YERKES-DODSON LAW ("ARC OF ANXIETY")

The Yerkes Dodson Law, often informally called the Arc of Anxiety,[1] illustrates a relationship between arousal (or anxiety) and performance level (Figure 1.1). The model was developed by the psychologists Robert M. Yerkes and John Dillingham Dodson in 1908 and is effective for explaining and illustrating how too much—or too little—anxiety interferes with performance. The inverted U shape indicates how performance is enhanced—to a certain point—when there is some increased physical or psychological arousal. When levels of mental or physical arousal become too high,

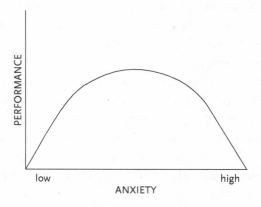

FIGURE 1.1 Yerkes Dodson Law ("Arc of Anxiety")

[1] Yerkes, R. M., & Dodson, J. D. (1908). The relation of strength of stimulus to rapidity of habit-formation. *Journal of Comparative Neurology and Psychology, 18,* 459–482.

performance competence decreases. Further, an absence of anxiety (or too little arousal) also leads to a decrease in performance proficiency. Arousal is defined as mental energy. It may be helpful for teachers to use the "spice" analogy in explaining this concept to students.

Musicians often express the wish to totally eliminate anxiety in performance. This is understandable. As the Arc of Anxiety illustrates, this is not desirable. For example, if performers are sleepy, or do not care, or are unmotivated, performance will suffer. The same thing happens when the performer is too keyed up, highly anxious, and fearful. Both high and low anxiety can result in a poor performance. A moderate and manageable level of anxiety (energy, spice, and fire) is necessary for optimum performing at one's personal best. A key element is to strive for one's personal best, not some magic goal of perfection or imitation of another admired performer. Appreciation of one's personal best is an important lesson for music teachers to convey to students, and this lesson needs to be continually emphasized. It asserts that *attitude* can facilitate anxiety reduction as much as, or sometimes more than, *aptitude*.

Biologically, the brain and adrenal glands produce chemicals in the body that are sensitive to stress. Common stress hormones include epinephrine (also known as adrenaline), norepinephrine, and cortisol, which function as neurotransmitters and hormones. If one experiences or perceives a physical or emotional stressor such as performance anxiety, there is an increase in hormonal activity. Anxious performers become keenly aware of cold hands, shaking fingers, increased perspiration, lowered concentration, rapid heartbeat, and other physical symptoms. Blood flow is directed away from the extremities, such as fingers and toes, toward the larger organs such as the heart. This "flight or fight" response prepares the body for battle, as though performance is a life-threatening experience.

What is emphasized here is that anxious mental attitudes and stress reactions convey a signal to the brain. The brain responds according to the chemical information it receives. The normal production of stress hormones and neurotransmitters is increased with intense and chronic stress. Prolonged stress is believed to lead to serious health problems such as diabetes, high cholesterol, gastrointestinal problems, suppression of the immune system, cardiovascular disease, and other conditions. The body/mind connection is powerful. It is important for musicians to get an adaptive handle on their stage fright stressors as soon as possible.

MENTAL PREPARATION: ATTITUDES AND APTITUDES

What is the "best" level of anxiety for optimum performance? Each person is different. There is not a "one size fits all" formula or single, simple solution for this stage fright question. Each person is unique and has distinctive triggers. There is no recipe. It is important to avoid comparing oneself with what others do or say. What works for one person may not be right for another person. Teachers can assist students develop an understanding of this important principle. It will help a great deal.

Teachers naturally help their students focus on how to practice by learning notes, rhythms, phrasing, and fingerings accurately. Teachers and students also talk about composers and analyze how the music is constructed theoretically. An important nonmusical component should be added to the pedagogical toolbox that helps students tune in to their feelings. Discussion of stage fright in the studio can do this and, over time, enhance confidence on stage.

Talent and fame are no guarantee of comfort and security on stage. Many famous performers have struggled with performance anxiety. Some have been sidelined by fears or chosen to discontinue playing in public. Regardless of how well prepared or experienced, there is a certain level of "unknown" about what will happen when going from back stage to center stage. Performers try very hard to be in control. That is one reason why students practice so hard. Yet hours of technical preparation may not offer emotional security in public performance. Mental preparation is as crucial as repertoire preparation.

There are no guarantees that intensified practicing will lead to an emotionally and technically secure performance. Of course, teachers help students practice intelligently and effectively, but there is no such thing as a perfect performance. Perfection is a "magic" wish that ultimately will raise anxiety, since perfection is unattainable. But a lack of perfection does not mean that there cannot be satisfying, good, and exceptional performances. Performance anxiety does not have to undermine or intimidate performers. When teachers emphasize that students do not have to strive for magical performances and "perfection," students' anxiety levels often drop significantly. Students can be encouraged to enjoy sharing their talent, the music itself, and the fruits of their hard work. An emphasis on *sharing*, rather than *proving*, has provided significant anxiety relief to many performers.

Managing anxiety begins with helping students develop performance *attitudes* that accompany their musical *aptitudes*. This can be worked on, along with repertoire, at any age. I have frequently heard comments suggesting that talking about performance anxiety makes it worse, but this is not true. This is "magical thinking," a term psychologists use to connote the belief that thinking about something literally makes the thought come true. Performance anxiety must not be a forbidden feeling or topic. No feeling or thought is forbidden. Emphasis should be placed on the difference between thinking and feeling and acting on feelings and thoughts. Performance anxiety begs for informed discussion in the teaching studio. Teachers and students should not be bullied, sabotaged, or imprisoned by it.

Discussing performance anxiety in the teaching studio in an intelligent, sympathetic, and informed manner is reassuring and emotionally calming. Such discussions indicate to students that teachers can handle tough topics and feelings, and these discussions convey the belief that students can too.

TALKING AND LISTENING TO STUDENTS: VALIDATING FEELINGS

Since many students begin piano lessons at a young age, teachers are in a position to address performance anxiety and minimize stress at a time when a child's mind is very open, flexible, and developing. Normalizing performance anxiety is an effective antidote to include in the teacher's and performer's musical and mental toolbox.

A young inexperienced student may tell you that she is scared before her first recital. It is a compliment to the teacher that the student is comfortable enough to share this information. This is a good time to initiate a discussion about scary feelings and performing. Most importantly, the teacher needs to listen to the student, not rationalize or attempt to diminish the student's feelings, and to take the student's concerns seriously. The student needs to feel understood and to hear the teacher comment that feeling scared is not "silly or stupid." The teacher needs to ask the student what she is afraid of, and what the student thinks might happen. The teacher should *not* reassure the student that everything will be fine. The student is scared; everything is not fine. Rather than address the student's anxiety rationally from the teacher's perspective, the teacher must respond to the heightened emotional message the student is conveying. Responding to the student's affect, the teacher allows the student to feel understood and conveys that the student's feelings are real. It is important to remember that when dealing with anxious students, validating affects first is much more effective than offering reason and technical solutions. Every student, regardless of age or experience, needs to be "heard" on an emotional level.

It is helpful for the teacher to be empathetic, and to let the student know that the teacher is glad the student could share her feelings. The teacher can ask the student to describe how she feels when she is scared and inquire when and where the student has been scared before. The teacher can ask how the student dealt with her nerves in the past. This allows the teacher to help her student articulate her feelings and discover that the teacher is listening carefully. The student, who may feel ashamed of her anxiety, will realize that the teacher is not afraid of the student's strong emotions, will not embarrass the student, and can talk about feelings. The student's notion of being "perfect" is softened by an inquiring attitude. Only when there is a level of trust and communication between teacher and student can technical, musical, and performance problems be addressed effectively.

What is most important is to listen, keep communication open, and convey that no thought or feeling is forbidden or bad. The goals are to help the student trust the teacher as an important, trusted caregiver (and welcoming "audience"), and for the student to eventually believe that she is good enough to feel competent. Perfection is never the goal.

One way that the teacher can offer help is to talk with the student about how the student has found solutions in past nonmusical situations when the student was nervous (e.g., during a test, a speech, writing a paper, a social event.) If one musical issue is fear of having a memory slip, the teacher can talk with (and listen to) the student about the student's fear of looking stupid or feeling humiliated in front of family and friends. As an example of one coping method, once a discussion has been initiated, the teacher could indicate that it is OK to keep the music open on the piano. Teachers should not underestimate the importance of helping students identify feelings and transform them into words.

It is essential for the teacher to realize that as the student separates from the teacher, the security of the studio, and moving from back stage to being alone performing on stage, the student is coping with the earlier developmental task of separation from parents and assertion of herself independently in front of others who are in the audience. Thus, the teacher needs sensitively to assist the student incorporate pedagogical and psychological techniques that help the student accomplish this endeavor while facilitating security and safety inside the student's mind. Toward this end, repertoire should be appropriate so that the music is not beyond the student's technical and emotional capacity. The recital music should be ready long before the recital. Should the student not respond to the teacher's efforts to help, it may be better to allow the student to watch the recital or play first, so the student does not have to sit, stew, and wait for a long period of time before performing. Worth emphasizing, the teacher needs to help the student over time, not just at the point of a recital, to develop healthy self-esteem and pleasure in performing so that recitals are events to anticipate, enjoy, and not fear.

IMPLICATIONS FOR MUSIC TEACHERS

- Demonstrate openness and willingness to talk with students, and communicate nonjudgmental attitudes when talking about performance anxiety.
- Be an attentive listener to students' words and body language.
- Inform students it is not desirable to totally get rid of performance anxiety—and why.
- Use the Yerkes-Dodson ("Arc of Anxiety") graph to illustrate how anxiety can work for optimum (not perfect) performances.
- Challenge and discuss the use of the word "perfect."
- Emphasize the idea of *sharing* music versus *proving* oneself when performing.
- Impress on students and parents that performance anxiety does not just start when the student goes on stage. Stage fright has a long incubation in the student's life history.

2

DELVING DEEPER

INTO STAGE FRIGHT

QUESTIONS FOR THOUGHT

- What are some physical sensations and emotional reactions that occur when students are anxious?
- What are three ways students may express anxiety?
- What are symptoms?
- How can teachers help students recognize anxiety symptoms?

STAGE FRIGHT:
A MIND-BODY DUET

Performers frequently ask if there is a brief answer for eliminating stage fright. The briefest answer is *no*. Stage fright does not develop overnight. It is not remedied quickly or without effort.

Typically people experience anxiety as psychological and/or physical uneasiness, terrifying panic attacks, and sometimes as physical pain, injury, and other forms of physical distress such as stomachaches, headaches, cold hands, and shakiness. These feelings are often accompanied by thoughts or cognitions about failing, exposure as inadequate in front of others (audience, teachers, friends, parents), being made fun of, and, worst of all, being dismissed as inadequate. Who has not known the self-doubts and "what ifs" that creep into one's mind with catastrophic thoughts before, during, or after a performance? These thoughts, or cognitions, which cast aspersions on one's competence and self-esteem, frequently are accompanied by physical discomforts such as those mentioned earlier and also including sweating, shaking, butterflies in the stomach, diarrhea, muscle rigidity, and sometimes pain in the specific part of the body that is used to play one's instrument. Pianists often experience limp fingers. String players fear shaking and dropping their bow, and wind players worry about their embouchure. Performance anxiety is very democratic, as it attacks all ages, experience levels, and seems to know what part of the body plays each instrument. These uncomfortable, and at times debilitating feelings, body sensations, and thoughts, are called symptoms. They are fueled by one's body/mind duet when one feels anxious.

SYMPTOMS OF PERFORMANCE ANXIETY

The body and mind are always in dialogue. Sometimes this duet is in tune; sometimes the duet is dissonant. Performance-anxious students are acutely sensitive and tuned in to their symptoms. Symptoms are not the cause of performance anxiety. They are the result of it. Students are understandably alarmed and distracted by anxiety symptoms—which, of course, take concentration away from efforts to focus on the music that has been prepared carefully with teachers.

Stage fright symptoms make students feel embarrassed or ashamed, and students often take measures to cover up anxiety by not talking about it at all or appearing as though it's "no big deal."

During a concerto competition at a prestigious music school, one contestant said to another (just before going on stage), "I'm going to beat you up in this competition." This performer (no doubt anxious himself) was using the technique of trying to "psych out" his competitor by adopting the attitude, "I don't care, performing does not bother me, and I am going to win." Teachers must prepare students for the psychological tactics they encounter from others, help students stay focused on music and developing a good sense of unique self-worth that is resistant to intimidation.

Many students feel that performance anxiety is a flaw that should be kept "secret" but, worse, that everyone in the audience will discover it. Naturally, students do not want this "truth" to be discovered in front of others, they feel psychologically threatened in a dangerous situation, and they experience anxiety symptoms. Performance anxiety descends on students, and on all performers, at the worst possible time—just when one has to play. In reality, performance anxiety begins off stage. Playing in a recital ignites anxiety that may be asleep when the stressors of performing in public are not imminently present.

DISCUSSING PERFORMANCE ANXIETY IN STUDIO CLASS

The studio class can be a wonderful place to try out performance pieces and performance nerves. It is also a good venue to talk about what performers feel, and for the teacher to address the idea that stage fright is a natural emotion that can be used as energy to fuel a performance. This kind of open dialogue and teacher understanding will deflate some of the negative power of anxiety. Teachers can help students understand that stage fright is a clue, or symptom, that warns one that it is time to use psychological coping methods from a mental toolbox.

It is not difficult to establish a norm for talking about performance anxiety in studio classes. Students expect feedback from the teacher about performances. During the discussion of students' performances, the teacher could ask some questions about how the student felt before playing and while playing. How has he dealt with his feelings? What suggestions would the student give others about feeling nervous? What helped the most? What was unhelpful? The topic could be opened up for general discussion with other students who also are invited to share their experiences. Preferably, the teacher would have first talked about these issues during lessons so that exploring the topic of performance in class would not feel threatening or unusual. Talking about performing, including anxiety, becomes the norm, not the exception.

This kind of dialogue should feel natural and comfortable for both teachers and students. If there are reasons why talking about performance anxiety does not feel safe, they should be explored. The teacher must create an open and respectful environment for such discussions and be comfortable talking about uncomfortable topics. The teacher needs to let students know that what is discussed is respected, and emphasize that what may work for one person is not necessarily going to be helpful for another.

Depending on the age of the student, some students will feel more comfortable talking about feelings. Some will be more comfortable talking about what they think. It is helpful to discuss the differences between feelings and thoughts and how they work together.

No one should feel pressure to talk (or "perform.") If students are not comfortable talking about their anxieties, teachers should not push them but rather acknowledge how hard it is to do this. People also learn through listening. Teachers can suggest that maybe at another time some students can contribute to the discussion. If the teacher is comfortable with the topic of performance anxiety, this attitude will be transmitted to the students.

IDENTIFYING PERFORMANCE ANXIETY SYMPTOMS

The chart below lists some performance anxiety symptoms, which are helpful to identify for students in order to explain psychological discomforts. While anything can be a symptom (e.g., arriving late to lessons, forgetting to pay, not correcting notes), symptoms typically are categorized as psychological, physical, and/or cognitive (thoughts). Students can experience any symptom singly or be aware of many symptoms simultaneously. Teachers need to remember that symptoms are the overt manifestations of underlying anxiety. Symptoms are not anxiety. By understanding what fuels anxiety symptoms, teachers can be in a better position to assist students take charge of anxiety. It should be noted that the chart that follows is not inclusive of all symptoms.

Chart 2.1

SYMPTOMS	
Psychological (Emotions/Feelings)	*Physical (Body Awareness)*
I feel embarrassed.	My hands are shaking.
I fear humiliation.	My heart is beating quickly.
I feel helpless.	My hands are sweating.
I worry about audience reaction.	My stomach hurts.
I feel self-consciousness.	My chest is tight.
I fear my technique will not work	I cannot sleep.
I worry about memory slips.	My hands are cold.

Cognitions (Thoughts)
I will not play well.
My teacher/friends will not like me.
I know what they are thinking.
I will look stupid.
I will mess up.
I will be ashamed.
People will laugh at me.
I do not want to be in another recital.
I want to stop lessons.

It is worth reiterating that emotions, thoughts, and physical symptoms can be experienced singly and/or collectively at the same time, since the body and mind work together. The mind works contrapuntally, similar to many voices in a fugue being played together, although one may focus on a single melodic line at any time. As in fugal playing, the performer may be tuned into one aspect of the body and mind duet, or one may experience cognitions, feelings, and physical sensations simultaneously.

MOOD RING

To illustrate the body-mind interaction with a simple experiment, have students try on a "mood" ring, which can be found in many toy and department stores. As the student becomes aware of thoughts and feelings, watch the ring change color. Have the student sit quietly and do some deep, slow breathing for several minutes. The ring does not know what the student feels or why the student feels the way he does, but skin temperature, as measured by blood flow that reaches the extremities (fingers, toes) is reactive to emotions. The ring responds by changing color according to blood flow in the body, which, in turn, reacts to tension and relaxation.

Many are familiar with feeling the sensation of cold hands prior to a performance. This occurs as blood flows primarily to the large organs such as the heart and lungs. This physical response prepares one for what the mind perceives as a danger situation. (Our distant ancestors had the dangerous task of resorting to fight or flight when taming wild beasts, and they needed blood flowing to their large organs to help them flee or fight.)[1]

A recital often can be perceived by an anxious performer as a "battle," and the body will react accordingly. Cold fingers are distracting for concentration, and they inhibit the small muscles required to play instruments. Therefore, fingers, sometimes toes—the extremities—will have less blood flowing toward

---

[1] Nagel, J. J., Himle, D. P., & Papsdorf, J. (1989b). Cognitive behavioral treatment of musical performance anxiety, *Psychology of Music, 17*. This last reference addresses the issue of blood flow and anxiety and implies that behavioral strategies and pharmacological techniques for lowering anxiety are indicated. These strategies can be helpful for some individuals. The reader will note in subsequent chapters that there are theories and therapies, in addition to behavioral models, that successfully address anxiety symptoms and anxiety reduction and examine the underlying roots of anxiety development.

them. In the experiment, the "mood" ring reflects the body/ mind connection in a colorful—although not scientific—way. There is research to support this simple illustration of cold/ warm hands, and the effects of anxiety on the body.

CHILL OUT!: TOOLS FOR "COOL" STUDENTS

This section illustrates the benefits of "chilling out" (or calming down) when one wants to "warm up." In other words, when a person practices deep, slow breathing and relaxation, the brain sends a message to the fingers to become warmer. This mental activity will also help students feel calmer emotionally when they are anxious. This activity has a few variations, described here, that can be added to the rhythmic breathing once it is mastered.

Deep Breathing

1. *Breathe In* through your nose on the count 1, 2, 3, 4 *Hold* your breath and count 1, 2, 3, 4 *Breathe out* through your slightly open lips and count 1, 2, 3, 4 Do this 4 times.
2. Deep Breathing, as above, but adding relaxing images in your mind such as a beach, a winter scene, a favorite holiday event, a cuddly pet, a warm blanket.
3. Deep Breathing, as above, and imagining your performance being successful (play a "visual"— mental—recital in your mind.)

Progressive Muscle Relaxation

Tense one muscle at a time and then release it (do one side of the body and then the other) starting with your feet and working up the body to your legs, torso, arms, and face. Hold each muscle tightly for a count of 4 and release tension all at once. When tensing, focus your attention on that tense muscle. When relaxing the muscle, focus attention on the relaxed muscle.

Notice and feel the difference between tense muscles and relaxed muscles.

Take your time and pay attention to each muscle group as you tense, hold, and release.

Notice if your hands begin to feel warmer by the end of this exercise.

It is important to practice breathing and relaxation exercises regularly, as one practices an instrument, for the exercises to become effective when needed to deal with anxiety. Teachers must emphasize this with students and not wait until anxiety strikes just before a recital.

IMPLICATIONS FOR MUSIC TEACHERS

- Appreciate the body-mind dialogue.
- Realize that for every physical issue (pain, injury) there are psychological implications (worry, lowered self-esteem, embarrassment).
- Sensitize students to the idea that stage fright complaints are expressed through symptoms.
- Understand that symptoms are expressed through physical, emotional, and cognitive communications.
- Use "chill out" tools from the mental tool kit to help students; these include deep breathing, imagery, and progressive relaxation.

3

THE A B Cs OF STAGE FRIGHT

QUESTIONS FOR THOUGHT

- What is an irrational thought or feeling?
- Why isn't advice and positive thinking sufficient to reduce stage fright?
- How can teachers help students recognize the anxious feelings, thoughts, and body sensations that are involved in performance anxiety?

The advice "practice harder" or "don't worry" will not reduce performance anxiety. Some people suggest that one should change *irrational, negative,* and *self-defeating* thoughts into positive statements. Thinking positively is commendable, intense focused practice is necessary, and "don't worry" may be reassuring, but frequently none of this advice is sufficient for performance success. There is no such thing as an "irrational" thought or feeling. What typically is labeled an "irrational" thought is often is an idea or strong feeling that needs to be better understood.

All thoughts and feelings have unique meaning for each person, but sometimes one is not fully aware of what he is thinking and feeling. Too often, anxiety is experienced as a reaction to thoughts and feelings. Strong emotions are best understood rather than labeled "rational" or "irrational." Multiple factors fuel thoughts and feelings that are experienced as anxiety and symptoms. Teachers need to talk with students about what is bothering them. Symptoms are a clue that a thought or feeling is troublesome and should not be buried in mental sand. Most helpful is to identify first what the student is worrying about, talk about it with the student, and then empathize and discuss the general idea that worry is distressing to the extent it could undermine talent and good practice habits. The teacher then can offer practical ways to deal with worry and anxiety as antidotes to stressors. Musical instruction should be combined with discussions about music performance anxiety, which communicates simple information that conveys how anxiety can be better understood. This offers the student a way to feel that she can regain control when feelings seem out of control and scary.

AN A B C MODEL OF ANXIETY

An A B C model to conceptualize anxiety responses was developed by the American psychologist Albert Ellis (1913–2007) as a self-help and clinical tool to help people identify and understand what Ellis called "irrational" thoughts and feelings. Ellis recommended challenging and replacing negative and irrational thoughts with positive alternatives. While this model is associated with rational emotive behavior therapy (RET), it is applicable to other situations, such as teaching and different therapeutic models. Using the A B C tool for identifying anxiety is an important way teachers can conceptualize and help students recognize feelings, thoughts, behaviors, and body sensations that accompany performance anxiety. This recognition can lead to identifying and discussing thoughts and feelings that may raise—but also can lower—anxiety and stress levels.

The letters A B C refer to an identified situation and the emotional and cognitive reactions to that situation. For example, Letter A = a recital. Anticipating a performance, an anxious student may experience a body sensation (muscle tension, shaking) or thoughts/cognitions ("I am afraid I will have a memory slip"), and/or a feeling/affect (fear, panic) that raises anxiety and stress. The thoughts, feelings, or physical sensations are identified by what the student says, feels, and is consciously aware of, and are represented by Letter B. The outcome of a performance is represented by Letter C (feeling ashamed/proud, dreading performance/enjoying performance, shaking muscles/calm muscles).

This ABC model is used in various ways throughout the rest of this book and applied to several psychological models. Particular emphasis is placed on Letter B throughout, so it is important to understand this concept. While one cannot control the existence of recitals (Letter A), one can become aware of one's personal bodily reactions, thoughts, and feelings (Letter B). As teachers help students become aware of their reactions (Letter B), teachers will be able to help students realize how anxiety is raised and lowered by tuning in and paying attention to oneself. By helping students recognize reactions that originate in their own mind and body (Letter B), the consequences of anxiety (Letter C) can be managed more effectively.

RECAP: A B C MODEL

A = an important event such as a recital or audition
B = thoughts (cognitions), feelings, body sensations
C = outcome of recital, audition, jury

While performance has many difficult external issues associ-ated with it (e.g., cold room, out-of-tune piano, poor light-ing), it is suggested that teachers assist students in realizing that anxiety and stress have psychological and emotional triggers *inside* their mind that shape their attitudes and feel-ings. Teachers can remind students that their most powerful instrument is the mind. Often, anxiety is experienced as a subjective, mystifying, and unformulated reaction. By learn-ing to identify specific thoughts, feelings, and physical reac-tions (Letter B), students and teachers can have productive conversations and devise effective coping strategies. A per-former cannot change the temperature of the room or the noise in the hallway, but the performer can better under-stand her feelings and thoughts that originate inside her mind about temperature and noise. Self-control is related to mental control and not worrying about controlling external factors beyond one's control.

It is important to keep Letter B in mind as you read this book. Thinking about performance anxiety in terms of this important letter will be a guiding leitmotif through most of the chapters.

Vignette: John

John has an audition ("A") for the local music teachers' organi-zation competition. He has practiced hard, and both he and his teacher feel that he is ready to perform.

John tells himself that he is afraid of having memory slips, and that if he does, he will disappoint his teacher as well as his parents, and he will be a failure ("B"). He fears losing status among his friends and will feel humiliated.

The day of the audition, John woke up with a bad headache and was shaking when he walked on stage. His performance suffered, as did his self-esteem. He had memory and technical "accidents" on stage and felt embarrassed and ashamed. He was also confused, because he was well prepared musically (C). John's teacher cannot simply tell him that this was just an unlucky day. John feels devastated. His teacher feels perplexed about how to help him.

John experienced both psychological and physical symptoms that accompanied his self-doubting thoughts ("B"). Anxiety over public performance became so debilitating that it covered up John's preparation and talent. His teacher also had many thoughts ("B") about what happened, but felt limited in the type of help she could offer. This type of situation can result in an impasse in the teaching studio and frustration for both teacher and student.

ACTIONS FOR TEACHERS AND STUDENTS

The following activities will assist teachers and students learn to identity Letter B responses and use them productively.

Activity 1—Identifying Letter B Responses

The teacher will help students identify Letter B responses. For John, his Letter B included both physical and emotional reactions (headache and shaking), as well as fears of memory slips in performance. The teacher could offer help both in lessons and in studio classes. At first, the teacher would point out how the student used unhelpful (anxiety) statements. Then the teacher could offer a range of supportive self-statements (Letter B), which can lower anxiety. Over time, students could be asked to think about anxiety-promoting responses and then to generate anxiety-lowering statements (Letter B). Consequently, students will become tuned in to the use of their mind regarding mental reactions to performance while experiencing an increasing sense of personal control over anxiety.

Example of *unhelpful* responses for Letter B (which raise anxiety)

- I am afraid I will have a memory slip and forget my music.
- I do not want to look stupid if I mess up.
- I do not play as well as my friend plays.

Examples of *revised* helpful responses for Letter B (which lower anxiety)

- I have prepared and practiced intelligently.
- I have good reasons to believe I will perform well.
- It is time to trust myself.
- I cannot guarantee everyone will like my playing, even when I play my best.
- I will do my best.
- The audience is coming to support me.
- The audience is not coming to judge me. I must not judge myself.
- I need not compare myself with anybody else.
- Everyone plays differently.

Activity 2—Letter B Cards: Supportive Self-Statements

Teachers can hand out cards to students with supportive statements that lower anxiety.

Invite students to generate some of their own supportive Letter B statements.

Invite students to "coach" other students with supportive Letter B statements in studio classes.

Discuss supportive Letter B statements with students.

Examples of Supportive Self-Statements

- Focus on what you are playing in the moment.
- Trust your brain. Focused practice leads to more confident performing.
- Trust that you can recover from mistakes and keep going.
- Give yourself permission to make a mistake and not conclude that you have failed.
- Do not judge yourself if you make a mistake.
- Consider the instrument as your friend—give it a name.
- Do not judge others or compare yourself to anyone else.
- Use breathing exercises both on and off stage. Practice them daily.
- Visualize that your recital is successful (away from the piano) before going on stage.
- Practice mindfully. Focus on what you are playing at the moment.
- Fix mistakes as you practice (otherwise your brain will send you signals to repeat music that you have learned incorrectly).

- Play your pieces all the way through (after you have fixed your mistakes).
- Develop a "jam plan" for when you make mistakes in a recital.
- Learn to recover from mistakes without stopping (use your "jam plan"—for example, prepare a measure where you can start again or move to another section).
- Carry Letter B cards to your recitals.

IMPLICATIONS FOR TEACHERS

- Realize that all thoughts (cognitions) and feelings are important.
- Understand the A B C model regarding anxiety.
- Emphasize the importance of Letter B.
- Help students identify their Letter B statements/symptoms.
- Point out that students' thoughts and self-statements can raise or lower anxiety (Letter B).
- Assist students in relabeling unhelpful Letter B statements into supportive Letter B statements
- Invite students to generate Letter B coping statements.

4

SYMPTOMS

Elimination vs. Management

QUESTIONS FOR THOUGHT

- What is a symptom?
- How can the teacher help students understand that anxiety is a symptom?
- How can symptoms of anxiety be useful for students and teachers?
- What are internal (inside the mind) and external (social, environmental) triggers for anxiety?
- Why is it important to validate students' feelings?
- What is paradoxical about the conflicts that are inherent in performance anxiety?
- What are "jam plans," and how does the teacher help students develop them?
- How is performance anxiety related to other issues in the student's life?
- Why is it important for teachers to monitor their own emotional responses to students?

SYMPTOMS AS CUES AND CLUES

Awareness of a feeling or thought that makes one uncomfortable (or comfortable) and worried (or happy) is a signal or symptom (Letter B). Signals, also called symptoms, when troublesome, are psychological warnings about a perceived "danger" situation. The experience of performance anxiety is determined by troublesome, uncomfortable symptoms. Signals and symptoms are invitations from the mind to examine what the student is feeling. Signals and symptoms can lead to discussion, self-reflection, and productive problem-solving.

There are effective ways to deal with performance anxiety symptoms, but teachers should not have a goal of eliminating a student's performance anxiety entirely. This is both impossible and undesirable. It is important to keep in mind that it is not the presence or absence of symptoms that contribute to performance anxiety. It is rather the degree to which anxiety is bothersome, how often anxiety is experienced, how severely it interferes with performance and self-esteem, and whether stage fright prevents enjoyment in living and in performing.

Teachers can help students understand that there are a range of anxiety responses and compare this to expressing a range of musical dynamics when playing an instrument. Students can experiment playing soft and playing loud (as well as experimenting with numerous other dynamics) on their instrument or voice to realize that there are nuanced varieties of sound. So, too, is there a wide range of feelings. Anxiety symptoms vary for each individual, so it is important for teachers to help students stop comparing themselves with others who react differently.

Teachers need to emphasize that it is neither good nor bad to feel anxious in performance. It is normal to experience anxiety. It is essential not to be judgmental about oneself or others. Anxiety can be a cue to employ mental tools, and can be used as positive energy to facilitate improving self-esteem, so important to playing in public. One of the most important things for teachers to convey about anxiety is that there are a number of effective ways students can cope with stage fright.

Compare the signal of performance anxiety to the example of using a thermometer. A fever is a signal that some physical process is going on inside one's body that needs attention. It is *not* a sign that one is bad. Yet often, students believe there is something "bad" or "wrong" with them when their stress level is high and they feel anxious.

The most helpful approach for reducing performance anxiety symptoms is to understand why students experience self-doubts, and what they fear about what others (including the teacher) think. Teachers will discover that students' feelings and thoughts (Letter B) often involve anxiety about looking stupid and feeling ashamed or embarrassed. These are powerful feelings.

There is no thought or feeling that is irrational. Every thought and feeling is a clue for detective work and further evaluation and understanding. Much of what is subjectively experienced as anxiety typically is outside of one's conscious awareness. Each person is unique and has meaningful experiences starting in infancy that are unlike anyone else's in the world. A cold room will bother some people but not others. Some students cannot eat before a performance while others enjoy meals for energy. Some students experience teacher comments as criticism; others hear comments as supportive. The short vignette that follows illustrates how both internal and external events led to symptoms that shaped a student's cognitions, feelings, and bodily awareness.

Vignette: Cindy

Cindy was a pianist who always had cold hands before a performance and was acutely aware of the temperature of the concert hall. She said she could not play well or feel comfortable when the room was cold.

When she was a child, her parents had many squabbles and eventually divorced. Cindy lived with her mother, who was depressed and did not have the energy to devote to her daughter's feelings about the breakup of the family. Cindy began playing the piano for comfort and became quite accomplished. But she could not understand what she believed was her mother's "coldness" toward her. She had the persistent thought that she had been responsible for the divorce and that her behavior was the reason why her mother was emotionally chilly. Cindy unknowingly associated her mother's coldness with her cold hands. Both her feelings and thoughts were reflected in her performance anxiety symptoms.

Many years later Cindy realized that playing the piano to calm herself in childhood and being sensitive to the cold (room temperature, cold hands, and mother's moods) were connected through her symptoms. Cindy had nothing to do with the divorce or her mother's depression, which Cindy experienced as coldness toward her.

The awareness of coldness had great meaning for Cindy, which could be triggered by a cold room (external trigger—room temperature) or cold hands (internal trigger—physical sensations) or fears about a "cold" audience reaction (cognitions and emotions about rejection). Students bring a life history into lessons and onto the stage, but their history becomes disguised from its original source that typically has roots earlier in life. Disguised emotions and cognitions typically surface as symptoms.

ASSESSING THOUGHTS
AND FEELINGS

Thoughts and feelings in the context of symptoms must be assessed as carefully as musical technique. Awareness of the student's thoughts and feelings is an important tool in the teacher's mental toolbox. It is no small accomplishment for teachers to communicate with students and to develop a trusting relationship with them so that anxiety can be explored. Because students feel embarrassed about their self-doubts, it takes time, patience, and tact to establish this atmosphere in a relationship. The effort is worth it.

Knowledge and awareness about students' thoughts and feelings allows movement to the next step in helping them deal more effectively with stage fright. By identifying symptoms and realizing that symptoms are signaling a special message about worries, doubts, and fears, students and teachers can become aware that *all feelings and thoughts contain meaning and messages*. This realization is the foundation for the development of control over frightening feelings and gradually helps lower performance anxiety. Self-awareness cannot be skipped. At times, a professional consultation will be helpful to unravel persistent symptoms that are debilitating.

Many students believe that performance anxiety is caused by something beyond one's control—such as the temperature of the room, a piano with hard action, poor lighting, or that the audience will be a harsh judge. Some rooms are too cold; some are too hot. Some people in an audience will not like a performance no matter how well the music is played. And, there are many inferior instruments, particularly when the student is a pianist and cannot choose the instrument. All of these things, and many others, do have an effect on performers, but in themselves do not *cause* performance anxiety. It is important to help students deal adaptively with external situations that are less than optimal and that cannot be changed. Students can learn that they can alter their internal reactions, which include their thoughts and feelings. Ultimately, this realization helps them to deal more effectively with their emotional reactions, no matter what occurs in the external environment.

TALKING ABOUT STRESSORS

The mind registers both obvious and subtle clues about performance anxiety. How students' minds, bodies, and feelings respond to external situations such as playing in public can either *interfere* with performance or *assist* with performance energy and increased self-esteem. Teachers can help students better recognize and regulate thoughts and feelings so that their minds can work for them when they are anxious.

Teachers can encourage their students to talk about symptoms (thoughts, feelings, body awareness—Letter B) that bother them when they have performance anxiety. While teachers should be aware that students' symptoms are related to life events other than playing an instrument, they should not explore the origins of symptoms with their students. Typically neither students nor teachers are aware of how attitudes originate. While teachers can help students cope significantly with emotional issues in the studio and performance, probing early memories and experiences is not within the teacher's training and expertise. However, it is very appropriate for teachers to help students normalize stressful reactions that are related to performing and to identify and validate all feelings as ways to better manage (not eliminate) performance anxiety rather than being overwhelmed by it.

IMPLICATIONS FOR TEACHERS

- Normalize the feelings of performance anxiety with students.
- Emphasize that performance anxiety is neither good nor bad.
- Help students realize that they can learn to better manage (not eliminate) performance anxiety.
- Identify and discuss symptoms.
- Emphasize that symptoms are cues to pay attention to feelings, thoughts, and physical sensations.
- Invite students to discuss an imaginary person who is performing and talk about how this "person" is coping with stage fright. Are there suggestions that could be made to help this "performer?"
- Try this activity at a private lesson or in a group situation.
- Repeat this activity with students regularly, because identifying anxiety symptoms can be both embarrassing and difficult.
- Encourage students to use A B C tools to manage stress before recitals or in other situations where they may experience anxiety such as tests, speeches, and writing papers, playing sports, or asking questions in class.

5

CONFLICT

A Paradox

QUESTIONS FOR THOUGHT

- Why would a student experience performance anxiety if the student practices intelligently and is talented?
- What is a conflict?
- What are some conflicts involved in performance anxiety?
- What is "magic" thinking?
- Why, and in what ways, do students "fill the gaps"?
- What should teachers listen for in order to recognize students' conflicts involving performance anxiety?

PARADOX: IDENTIFYING EMOTIONAL CONFLICTS

It appears paradoxical that a wish to perform coupled with good teaching, diligent practice, and talent can be undermined by performance anxiety. How and why does this paradox occur?

Performance anxiety is a multifaceted and complicated topic, just as each person is a multifaceted and a complex individual. Strong emotions can override intellect, talent, good teaching, and rational thinking. When talent, preparation, and performance anxiety are at odds with each other, one experiences emotional conflict. A conflict develops inside the mind when a *wish* (to perform) and a *fear* (of performing) coexist. One could musically label conflict as dissonant mental counterpoint and clashing polytonalities. In other words, one wishes to perform well on stage but is afraid of falling apart at the same time.

Conflict stems from a basic underlying wish to find audience approval and respect. This is very natural and healthy. However, this wish for approval by a student (i.e., signified by applause, winning an audition, getting high grades, teacher approval) is opposed by the fear that people will not appreciate the performance, which is then experienced as a personal rejection coupled with the affect of shame. This conflict, if not resolved emotionally, may convince the performer that looking "stupid" and feeling embarrassed in public is guaranteed at each performance. Such conflicts fuel and exacerbate performance anxiety.

Conflict creates a breeding ground in the mind for symptoms to develop. Teachers must be aware of what constitutes conflict and listen for signs of overt or subtle signs of conflict in students' comments and attitudes. As discussed in the previous chapters, the first step for teachers is to identify what students say and feel (Letter B) when they speak about performing or about themselves (Letter A). Conflict will be noted in Letter B statements and in other behavioral symptoms.

Conflict is normal, and it can be adaptive. Conflict motivates all people. It can stimulate them to problem-solve. Conflict is the perpetual engine of mental life as people strive for emotional balance. When things go well, there is no awareness of conflict. But conflict can become obvious and interfere when people feel under pressure mentally and/ or from external sources. An internal psychological conflict occurs when performers become unsure of themselves, are doubtful of their competence, primarily depend on audience approval for self-esteem, and/or feel scared despite being prepared and choosing to perform. It is natural to feel confused and overwhelmed in such circumstances.

EXAMPLE OF CONFLICT

A nonmusical example of conflict (according to the ABC model) illustrates the concept when a student wants to stay up late to watch TV but knows going to bed early is important because he knows he has a test in school the next day. The student experiences conflict (Letter B) both within himself (internal) and between himself and his parents (external), who want him to go to bed. The student wants to do two opposing things at the same time—watch the late TV show and do well on the test!! Some activity or idea must be relinquished or modified, and a compromise must be worked out. This is reality. Staying up late results in the consequence of fatigue the next day (Letter C); getting enough sleep results in the consequence of feeling rested (Letter C). Both "solutions" have consequences (Letter C).

RECOGNIZING CONFLICTS

Conflict may be easily recognizable and identifiable, or it may surface as a nagging, uncomfortable feeling in the mind that appears without specific content. With performance anxiety, conflict typically centers on worries of negative evaluation in performance, fearing rejection, and feeling competitive with others. These feelings often are combined with worries about being exposed as inadequate, which lead to the affects of shame, humiliation, and embarrassment. Ultimately, conflict brings one face to face with the reality or fantasy of a fear of loss of self-esteem, shame, and audience disapproval. Conflict evokes extraordinarily powerful emotions, feelings, and behaviors that will be experienced in Letter B reactions.

While students are most aware and fearful of memory slips or technique meltdowns in recitals, it is important for teachers to keep in mind that the performer takes an entire life history that predates any performance onto the stage. The early age at which piano lesson are begun illustrates that both musical and psychological growth occur simultaneously, often leading the student to connect self-esteem with performance. For example, a good performance enhances self-esteem while a subpar performance (or perceived subpar performance) leaves performers feeling disgraced and/or questioning their ability and talent altogether. In the latter situation, subsequent performances become more stressful.

DEALING WITH MEMORY SLIPS AND TECHNIQUE MELTDOWNS

Teachers understandably may not be sure of the most helpful comment to make to a student who has experienced a memory slip while performing. In one way, the teacher is searching for the "perfect" comment, just as the student is searching for the "perfect" notes in performance. When possible, it is best for the student take the lead about how to approach this topic. The teacher must listen to the student calmly and carefully for subtle clues about self-condemnation and fears of inadequacy. Some students will want to talk, some will not. Teachers should consider whether the composition performed is newly learned, or if the repertoire presents unusual technical and musical challenges. With the safety of not feeling judged, the student will more likely confide in the teacher.

It is not advisable to reassure the student that it is all right, and that the student should not worry. This is not helpful, because the student is already upset and worried. It is precisely the worry that the student cannot manage, much less eliminate, on his own. Teachers also should not comment, "No one noticed." The student noticed. Self-esteem is threatened. What is most important is that the student be able to recover his or her "dignity" and not become phobic about future performances. The teacher can normalize the anxiety by suggesting, "memory slips happen, but there are ways to work together to learn how to recover from inevitable mistakes in performance." The teacher also needs to gently acknowledge the embarrassment the student probably experiences, even if the student does not say so directly. Recognizing affects helps diminish the student's own fear of strong feelings. It underscores that the teacher "understands" and will try to help.

At the lesson following a memory slip in performance, the teacher should go over the passage that was troublesome and analyze it musically and technically with the student. Encourage the student to perform soon again—in the next studio class, for example, so that the student does not harbor the painful memory for too long. The studio class is a good place to normalize memory slips for all students and to indicate it is acceptable to talk about them.

One helpful tactic for coping with memory slips is to develop jam plans, which are effective strategies students can use to recover from accidents. It is helpful for students to feel they have alternative pathways to regain control of the score and of their feelings, even if they lose control should memory fail and/or technique become unreliable on stage. It goes without saying that preparation is essential, but anxious emotions can override the best-prepared performance. Mental preparation is as crucial as musical preparation.

JAM PLANS

- Place the music on the piano stand when performing (even if student does not look at it).
- Use the music when necessary.
- Identify "safety zones" in the music where the student can recover and continue.
- Rehearse jumping to "safety zones" both using music and playing from memory.
- Encourage students not to give up.
- Remind students that there is no such thing as a "perfect performance."
- Work on helping students improvise music at lessons.
- Analyze the music harmonically and structurally so the student has more resources than tactile memory to rely on.
- Practice playing the music all the way through in a trial rehearsal, even with mistakes.

SOME CHILDHOOD
ANTECEDENTS OF STAGE FRIGHT

The strong feelings that are evoked by performing in public are related to the performer's personhood in many ways. This can include family, health, school, and social issues that the student has encountered during her early years or currently. For example, the student who has grown up in a dysfunctional or broken family may fear audience disapproval and abandonment while wishing for love and admiration (an example of conflict where a wish for love and fear of disapproval coexist). Similarly, if there have been losses such as deaths, illnesses, separations, moves in the family, and/or bullying in school, the student will have psychological scars, to a greater or lesser degree, that will accompany the student on stage at any age.

Losses and trauma in childhood need not be extreme or even obvious. People perceive all life events through different emotional lenses and with varying mental reactions. It is human nature to crave connectedness and approval. It is human nature to fear loss. All people are susceptible to fears of abandonment and criticism. Such fears often surface in performances of all kinds and include test anxiety, speech anxiety, social anxiety, writer's block, and/or academic anxiety. Particularly through music performance, the student may experience conflict about losing control on his instrument, signified by the symptoms of memory and technique loss. Conflict is also expressed around the issue of competition, which is ever-present from the earliest music lessons (local, state, and national) to entrance and performance juries at universities to professional national and international competitions. Both losing and winning competitions hold powerful psychological meaning for individuals, since all of us grow up in families with feelings about siblings, being favored by parents, and wanting to be special.

No one, despite positive or negative life circumstances, is immune from conflicts. Teachers must not convey any sense of judgment about conflicts noted in students. Conflict is a cue and warning from the mind to explore greater understanding of opposing impulses and attitudes. Understanding of opposing mental attitudes and mental compromise help reduce conflict's debilitating emotional power.

Conflict can be very useful. Life events have dynamic and profound meaning that can linger (although painful life milestones become buried deep inside the mind.) However, the mind never forgets. The mind "remembers" difficult conflicts particularly when one is under stress. Performance anxiety represents the emergence of stressful, often unresolved, conflicts that become ignited when performing before others.

ADDITIONAL EXAMPLES OF CONFLICT

Thinking developmentally, it is not unusual for a child who has experienced a family divorce to assume that it was because "he was bad and caused it to happen." Another child may believe that father's business trips took him away because father was mad at him. An adolescent who is starting to question parental attitudes and finding her own identity may feel guilty about betraying what her parents believe. This adolescent may worry that instead of abandoning parental norms, that the reverse will occur, namely, the parents will abandon the adolescent. Performers project these fears onto the audience, who, it is feared, will be rejecting and not loving. The variations on the conflicts of loss and competition are endless and very personally derived. In such situations, the need for perfection is heightened by the performer, because a fantasy persists that a perfect performance guarantees perfect love without loss (from audience and parents). These examples suggest that childhood family experiences are at the root of performance anxiety. This may or may not be true. Emphasis is strongly placed on the idea that it is not the presence or absence of difficult life experiences that creates conflict. Both how one deals with life's dilemmas and challenges, and how one is guided by caring others, including the music teacher, have powerful influence on all subsequent development.

Vignette: Robert

As Robert talked about his parents and his three siblings, it was clear that his parents were tuned in to his needs and encouraged his talent. One day, when Robert was eight years old, his mother needed to take a trip unexpectedly. Robert remained home with his two brothers, his sister, and his father. No one spoke about where his mother went, why she left, or when she would be home. Robert missed his mother terribly, but routines at home and school continued as usual. When she returned after several weeks, there was no discussion about her absence. Robert felt relieved to have her back and appeared very happy on the surface. But his mother now seemed sad and wept much of the time. Robert did not know why.

After some time had passed, the children were told that their favorite aunt had died, and their mother had gone to be with her because the aunt had been very ill. The parents were fearful of upsetting their children, so they did not speak of mother's absence with them.

The parents' avoidance of speaking about mother's absence and aunt's illness, in order to "protect" the children, did not do their children a favor. Yet, the parents handled the difficult situation in a way they believed was best. Now Robert also had to cope silently with the mysteries of loss and death; it had not been discussed at home. Now dealing with loss and his own sadness became more mysterious to him. From this time forward, Robert linked death and his mother's absence in his mind.

When Robert was older and performed in concerts as a music major at college, he found that he was so concerned with what others were thinking of his playing that he could not focus on what he was doing. He constantly worried that unexpected things would happen when he was on stage and he would have memory loss in performance. His memory slips and technical difficulties echoed another kind of early loss and anxiety, namely, the unexpected disappearance of his mother and loss of his beloved aunt. His stage fright, expressed through music performance as a symptom and an unresolved conflict, undermined him.

YOUNG CHILDREN (AND ADULTS) FILL THE GAPS

The human mind in people of all ages automatically and imaginatively fills gaps when attempting to explain confusing, conflicting feelings and life events in order to comprehend a complex world. Typically, such explanations are not reality based. Young children, in particular, commonly use "magic" thinking such as "the sun comes up in the morning so I can see to get dressed." They are naturally curious and relate everything to themselves. One young child became frightened when the electricity went out in her house during an electrical storm. She cried for her mother to "turn on the lights." The mother tried to explain, but could not possibly convince her toddler that she was unable to turn on the lights. When the electricity finally returned, the child exclaimed, "Good job! Mommy!!" The child magically attributed electricity returning to her mother's intervention. After all, young children assume both mother and father know best!

The young mind, not fully physically or psychologically developed, normally responds concretely and in a self-absorbed manner. The idea held by some children that an illness was caused by doing something about which the parents disapproved is another example of "magic" thinking. This was the case for Roslyn, who hid and ate her Halloween candy against her parents' wishes. When she developed severe abdominal distress years later, she remained convinced that her misbehavior with candy as a young child led to her stomach problems. She felt guilty and was not able to let herself play competently in recitals as a form of self-punishment. Roslyn was unable to accept the fact, emphasized by her parents and by her physician, that her current abdominal distress had nothing to do with eating candy as a child. By talking with a therapist, Roslyn was able to realize that her current GI problem had nothing concretely to do with her earlier mischievous behavior, but she had developed guilt that affected her self-esteem. She was able to stop feeling guilty, her stomach pain disappeared, and her performance anxiety diminished.

Beliefs established in childhood, such as those of Robert and Roslyn, feel very real to children, who construct meaning about themselves and their world when their minds are not fully developed. "Magic" thinking can affect self-esteem, motivation, one's frame of mind, and the formation of symptoms and conflicts of stage fright for years, long past an original event. While teachers (who become parents to their students symbolically through projections and displacements), cannot and should not try to ferret out the underlying dynamics of such attitudes, teachers can have an informed awareness of how the mind works to better understand that all behavior and all feelings are relevant. Appearing in a recital at any age can activate earliest life experiences from the student's earliest perspectives.

ADDITIONAL CONSIDERATIONS ABOUT CONFLICT

The charts below illustrate examples of conflicts that teachers and students can discuss. An awareness of conflicts will also help teachers and students better recognize and identify symptoms (Letter B). Notice how two differing thoughts or feelings dealing with evaluation, rejection, and competition are juxtaposed (i.e., wishes and fears), which are the hallmarks of a conflict. Also it is important to be alert to the idea that students can experience more than one conflict at a time.

The following chart is a recapitulation of symptoms, signified throughout this book by Letter B. An understanding of

Chart 5.1

CONFLICTS	
Wish	*Fear*
I want to play well.	I fear I will forget my music and technique.
Evaluation/Rejection	
I want approval.	I fear people won't like me.
Competition	
I want to win.	I fear I will mess up/lose
I want to be nice to others.	If I win, someone loses; I will feel guilty.

conflict enables the teacher to better identify the complexity of symptoms. As with conflicts, multiple symptoms typically can occur at the same time and provide clues to conflicts. Physical and psychological symptoms share many commonalities. It is important to rule out physical issues before attributing any symptom purely to psychological determinants.

Chart 5.2

SYMPTOMS	
Physical	*Psychological*
Shaking	Low self-esteem
Rapid heartbeat	Worries
Shortness of breath	Poor concentration
Sweating	Sleep problems
Abdominal distress	Appetite problems
Cold hands	Rejection worries

Physical and psychological symptoms are listed separately only for illustration here. Often multiple psychological symptoms are felt by the body, as the body "speaks" to the mind (remember the experiment using the mood ring) and the anxious mind speaks to the body (shaking, upset stomach, headaches, eating disorders, sleeping difficulties). It is important for teachers to pay attention both to physical and psychological symptoms, and to refer to a physician if physical symptoms are debilitating, chronic, and troublesome. Even if there is a physical diagnosis, there is always an emotional reaction regarding injury and illness to one's body.

Every student (and teacher) needs to feel special and learn to cope with fears of loss and competitiveness that are emotionally inherent in everyday life as well as in teaching and performing. It cannot be overemphasized that events such as deaths, losses, illnesses, separations, mistreatment, and changing homes, particularly in early childhood, have the potential to disrupt psychological equilibrium over the life span, unless help is offered when needed. In families where there are no overt problematic issues, it is still possible for children to grow up with various psychological needs and concerns. The music teacher can make relevant referrals and assist students with developing self-confidence and self-esteem as integral to healthy music making.

A word of caution for teachers, who also need to monitor their own emotional responses to students and within themselves. Competition frequently is experienced by students in the teaching studio as well as on stage. It is not unusual for students to want to be the teacher's "favorite," and some teachers may favor certain students subtly or overtly. Teachers also want to be singled out as exemplary by colleagues and other professionals by attracting good students and producing competition-winners and having large classes. Thus, teachers might (and do) feel competitive with other teachers. This is normal. However, if competition (or any feeling or thought) produces symptoms (Letter B) and emotional discomfort, both teachers and students need to take serious stock of themselves. Teachers will experience conflicts as they work with students and colleagues. This is inevitable, because teachers are human and conflicts are a normal part of mental life. Ideally, conflicts spark self-reflection and psychological growth. It is both necessary and effective for teachers to employ the ideas that they impart to their students regarding taking care of their own emotional needs.

IMPLICATIONS FOR TEACHERS

- Convey an open, nonjudgmental attitude to engage the student's trust.
- Appreciate that students bring an entire person with a life history into lessons and onto the stage.
- Understand that teachers often are first responders, hearing students' concerns about family, school, and friends.
- Emphasize to students that they will be sharing music without a need to prove how "fantastic" or "perfectly" they can play.
- Tune in to what students say and what students feel (Letter B), which can be viewed both as a symptom (Letter B) and/or a conflict (Letter B).
- Convey the relevance of "Letter B" in various contexts for use in students' performance anxiety "tool kit."

- Help students make a performance anxiety "tool kit" with Letter B statements.
- Emphasize that conflicts are normal and can be used for growth when understood.
- Become aware of one's own symptoms and conflicts.

6

THE EMOTIONAL FUEL BEHIND

STAGE FRIGHT

QUESTIONS FOR THOUGHT

- What does psychodynamic mean?
- How can psychodynamic ideas assist teachers understand stage fright?
- How can teachers use the concepts of displacement and transference to understand students' feelings and behavior?
- How can teachers better understand their own emotional reactions—or countertransference—toward students?
- How can teachers convey to students that the audience represents important authority figures (i.e., parents and significant others) in the student's life?
- How can teachers use Letter B to illustrate psychodynamic theory?
- Why is it important for teachers to understand the powerful emotion of shame as it is related to stage fright?

PSYCHODYNAMIC MODEL

Consideration of a student's overall psychological and physical development and family history are relevant in a discussion of performance anxiety. All people have a unique life narrative that is reflected in teaching, studying music, and performing. Life experiences *off* stage, beginning in the nursery, sit beside and inside every performer *on* stage. Teachers can benefit from knowledge of human development, particularly in the early years, to help them develop practical and effective strategies in the studio or classroom. Psychotherapists, like music teachers, have a number of theories and techniques for use in their metaphorical tool kit. These models of the mind help explain approaches to psychologically and musically informed teaching and performing. Several major psychological models that are useful for music teachers are explored as they pertain to helping students optimize mental security in performance.

The word "psychodynamic" illustrates the concept that the mind (*psyche*) and its mental energy are not static but are continually processing feelings and thoughts (*dynamic*). The mind is always active and never quiet, even (and particularly) during sleep. The brain and the mind are not identical. The brain is an anatomical structure in the body. It can be viewed and studied directly. The mind is not visible on scans and x-rays.

The mind represents mental energy that emanates from neurological functions and provides unique intrinsic meaning to all thoughts, feelings, and behaviors. Mental energy both motivates and inhibits all individuals according to their internal and external life experiences and perceptions. An fMRI[1] scan could demonstrate which area of the brain is active when an individual is anxious, or calm, or sad. This scan could not explain *why* an individual experiences anxiety, calmness, or sadness. Psychodynamic theory has developed clinical evidence to understand *meanings* associated with emotions and thoughts that cannot be seen directly, but nevertheless are felt deeply. The mental energy of the mind profoundly influences thoughts and behavior.

Earliest experiences, and the affects (emotions) that become attached to them, are the foundation of mental health and mental illness. All experiences and relationships carry emotional importance and are internalized by every individual. Sigmund Freud (1856–1939), trained as a neurologist, developed a comprehensive theory and treatment of the mind that probes the underlying motivations of mental functioning. Freud's revolutionary theory and treatment, psychoanalysis, is based on his research and clinical work that show thoughts and feelings outside (or lurking beneath) conscious awareness greatly influence observable feelings and behaviors.

Freud maintained that all people are significantly impacted by their earliest life experiences and/or fantasies about life experiences, many of which lie outside conscious awareness (i.e., in the *unconscious*). Clinically, significant relief from mental distress can be gained through talking with a professional trained in psychodynamic models. It is also possible for teachers, with some understanding of

[1] fMRI is the abbreviation for **functional magnetic resonance imaging**, which uses advanced MRI technology to measure blood flow and brain activity.

mental functioning short of psychological training, to play an important role in mediating students' emotional pain.

WHY CONSIDER PSYCHODYNAMIC MODELS OF THE MIND?

Freud stated

> In medical training you are accustomed to *see* things. You see an anatomical preparation, the precipitate of a chemical reaction, the shortening of a muscle as a result of the stimulation of its nerves. . . . even in many cases the agent of the disease in isolation. In the surgical departments you are witnesses of the active measures taken to bring help to patients. . . . Even in psychiatry the demonstration of patients with their altered facial expressions, their mode of speech and their behaviour, affords you plenty of observations which leave a deep impression on you. . . . In psychoanalysis, alas, everything is different. Nothing takes place in a psycho-analytic treatment but an interchange of words between the patient and the analyst. . . . The uninstructed relatives of our patients, who are only impressed by visible and tangible things—never fail to express their doubts whether "anything can be done about the illness by mere talking." . . . These are the same people who are so certain that are "simply imagining" their symptoms. . . . Words were originally magic and to this day words have retained much of their ancient magical power. By words one person can make another blissfully happy or drive him to despair, by words the teacher conveys his knowledge to his pupils, by words the orator carries his audience with him and determines their judgements and decisions. Words provoke affect and are in general the means of mutual influence among men. Thus we shall not depreciate the use of words in psychotherapy. (Vol. XV, p. 16–17.)

Freud's words about mental functioning are as relevant today as they were originally. The mind is invisible, but the mind also is transparent when one knows how to listen and respond to another person. While treatment does necessitate intense training, music teachers can employ some psychodynamic ideas in their studios.

MENTAL GHOSTS HAUNTING THE TEACHING STUDIO

While music teachers must never try to psychoanalyze their students, it is helpful for them to realize that talking about problems is helpful, and that the student's past influences the present, including the present relationship with the teacher and attitudes about performing before an audience. Painful feelings, memories, and fantasies become buried deep inside the mind but never vanish. As such, repressed feelings, memories, and fantasies in the unconscious can be reawakened by a variety of triggers, including anxiety about performance. The stimulus of performance can result in the emergence or reemergence of various symptoms (Letter B) and emotional conflicts (Letter B) many years after an original event has elapsed. To complicate matters, symptoms often appear in "disguise" to camouflage a vaguely recalled, misremembered (or misunderstood) occurrence or feeling that spawned them. Life experiences accumulate over the years and typically change perceptions by the time students struggle with performance anxiety. Teachers need to keep this in mind when students demonstrate stage fright.

Anxiety about what might occur (or fear of what might reoccur) in performance revives buried fears and/or fantasies. Unseen mental ghosts from the performer's past come alive on stage at the very time the performer wants and needs to be most competent. Talking openly about "mental ghosts" or "anxiety ghosts" with students can help to lower debilitating anxiety.

Freud also emphasized the significance of the body beginning at birth. Infants are soothed orally through being nursed and through skin sensations when coddled. Infants take in (internalize) the world initially through their eyes, ears, body, and tactile sensations. In good parenting, the child, who gurgles, coos, and cries, is responded to by an empathetic mother and caregivers. This nonverbal yet psychological and physical interaction with significant others sets the stage for all subsequent emotional development, and parenting plants seeds of having effective control over others who will respond lovingly. For performers, many years post-nursery, a positive interaction (applause, approval) is desired from the audience. Earliest affirmative interactions with another, particularly mother, lead to positive self-esteem, an antidote for performance anxiety.

At times, physical symptoms that are associated with stage fright may reveal what the mind conceals. Dependence on one's body to function properly and fears that it will not due to technical or memory slips are hallmarks of stage fright fears and psychological remnants from the past, since the body is one's first and most important instrument. Bodily malfunctions in public result in feelings of shame and embarrassment. These are feelings that are dreaded by everyone, and particularly by performers when in front of an audience. Phrases such as making "boo boos," "dropping notes," and "making a mess" are verbal expressions and not uncommon comments from performers who feel inadequate or complain about performance mistakes. The words to describe pre- and post-performance self-evaluations hearken back to very early stages of life, when body and mind were developing. Shame and embarrassment are typical affects that performers experience emotionally when feeling inadequate and small (in comparison to grown-ups and other performers with whom they may feel competitive).

THE MIND DOES NOT FORGET: THE UNCONSCIOUS

The concept of the unconscious is a bedrock principle of psychodynamic theory and treatment. Every person's mind functions automatically outside of conscious awareness. This may not be obvious to a performer or an observer. However, out of sight (or awareness) does not mean out of mind. The principle of unconscious functions of the mind actually helps to explain and reduce the mystery about why "trying harder," being "smart," "talented," "intellectual," and offering "advice" are not going to work for anxious students in the long run. Reassurance is helpful, to a point, and practice is absolutely necessary, but often self-help measures that address conscious awareness fall short, leaving teachers and students confused and frustrated.

The unconscious mental energy of the mind is our "mental underground." The unconscious is a repository of everything that one has ever experienced, perceived, fantasized, and felt affectively over a lifetime. According to psychodynamic theory, the unconscious is a primary source of psychological "fuel" that directs mental life twenty-four hours a day. If there have been difficult, misunderstood, or traumatic experiences in early childhood (deaths, divorces, separations, illness), the painful affects connected to such trauma will be buried in the unconscious. In one sense, buried psychological pain protects one from mental pain in the short run. Unfortunately, having a thought or feeling buried deep in the mind does not free one from its far-reaching effect. Thus the advice addressing intellect and rationality, "Don't think about it," literally is not possible. The mind is not like a faucet—it cannot be turned off. With help, painful experiences can be understood, and mental energy can be released for creative pursuits. While the unconscious never forgets, emotional pain can be modified and used for positive motivation. It must also be noted that pleasant events and feelings also are stored unconsciously and can provide antidotes to pain. However, pleasant life experiences and memories may not be immediately available when one is overcome and overwrought with anxiety.

One becomes aware of the unconscious through the emergence of conflicts and symptoms. This is complicated, however, because the unconscious disguises and distorts an original event from the past as well as the feelings attached to it. Cindy's cold hands were symptoms. Cold hands, her symptoms, were not the roots or cause of her stage fright. Her painful childhood trauma was her parents' divorce (which was remembered) and the unconscious guilt induced by Cindy's conviction that somehow she caused the family break-up to happen. Stage fright (a symptom) was one way Cindy unconsciously punished herself for her perceived, not real, transgression. Yet Cindy's feelings were real, and they needed to be considered seriously. No amount of reason and reassurance could eliminate her distress. Symptoms are one way the mind and body "remember" what the mind is also trying to forget. When mental material is buried deep below one's conscious awareness, it is repressed.

A VISUAL MODEL OF THE UNCONSCIOUS

Think of the illustration below as a pyramid or iceberg (Figure 6.1). The very small area in the top tip represents the **conscious** mind, which includes ideas, thoughts, and feelings of which one is aware. The largest area of the triangle connotes the **unconscious** mental energy of the mind, where ideas, thoughts and feelings are "buried," or repressed. The **preconscious** represents the mental space between the conscious and unconscious and suggests that some of the contents in our mental life are on the verge of coming into our awareness.

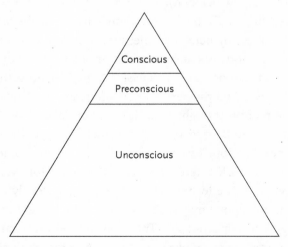

FIGURE 6.1 Conceptual Diagram of the Conscious, Preconscious, and Unconscious

One will notice immediately that most of the mind functions on the unconscious level. What is buried involuntarily in the unconscious depends on many factors inherent in an individual's emotional and genetic makeup. This may include each person's particular life story, physical resilience, the emotional supports received (or not received) from family and significant others, and all the subsequent events that occurred as the child grew older. The effect of life development is cumulative—similar to how a theme in a musical composition is presented in the exposition and how its fate, or development, occurs throughout the composition. When one speaks about how to understand performance anxiety from a psychodynamic perspective, one is referring to bringing material from the unconscious into conscious awareness and examining it in the present. When realizing that ancient feelings from childhood get repeated in current emotions and behaviors (necessary at one time when body and mind were not fully developed), one discovers how those feelings are working ineffectively and destructively in the present to prevent enjoyment and pleasure. Performance anxiety reflects a performer's unconscious fear of a repeat of dreaded affects and actions from one's past, and furthermore, that the audience will find the performer inadequate.

If a painful thought or feeling is buried very deeply in the unconscious, one typically cannot bring it into consciousness without some assistance. This is why some self-help books, while interesting, are *not* effective for everyone. However, if some feelings are not buried too deeply (in the preconscious), one may have an easier time retrieving them through self-help strategies. This is one reason why some self-help programs and books may be effective for some people. According to the psychodynamic model of the mind, when self-help, rational approaches and musical instruction do not produce positive results, emotional relief is best sought from working through (not merely identifying problems and offering advice) feelings and memories associated with past trauma and life events. This approach must be done with a professional therapist or psychoanalyst who has been trained specifically to conduct in-depth treatment.

REVISITING CINDY

Recall Cindy, who had cold hands. When Cindy was helped by her therapist to discover that "cold" held specific meaning for her, the feelings associated with her parents' divorce and the losses she experienced were explored (unconscious repressions made conscious), and she no longer harbored the myth lodged in her unconscious since childhood, that she had been the cause of their breakup. This realization was a tremendous relief for her. She come to understand that her ideas were actually "magic thinking," which is normal for a child. Therefore, Cindy no longer felt guilty and could use this knowledge to challenge and eventually dispel her childhood (not childish!) explanations. Over a period of time with her therapist's help, Cindy's deeper understanding of her parents' breakup enabled her to stop having breakdowns on stage, which symbolized her self-punishment for her childhood conviction of being a bad child. Cindy increasingly realized how the power of childhood fantasies and thinking was related to her stage fright.

Since musicians begin playing an instrument and taking lessons at young ages, childhood thoughts and feelings are very important for teachers to consider when thinking about performance anxiety. Children absorb everything that happens from tender ages. Children have curiosity and imagination. Children are not "too young" to be affected with anxiety and depression. Many adults maintain, "she's just a child, she is not understanding what we are talking about." While it is true that children do not understand events with adult perspectives, children fill gaps at their age level with very elaborate fantasies. How could children possibly have the ability to think on an adult level when they are not fully developed psychologically or physically? Yet children's' thoughts, experiences, feelings, and fantasies have lasting effects into adulthood.

Teachers do not need to be authorities in psychodynamic theory and therapy, but the importance of infancy and early childhood is crucial for teachers to comprehend in order to sensitively grasp the complexities that fuel students' stage fright. The "mental underground" works all the time, both on and off stage. According to psychodynamic theory, nothing in mental life occurs by chance or "accident." Thoughts and feelings have precedents and may become observable through symptoms and conflicts. Hidden meanings typically lurk beneath the overt surface. This awareness in itself is helpful for teachers to convey to students. The mind stores, projects, and displaces memories, fantasies, and feelings from the past about significant people onto individuals in the present such as teachers and audience members.

TRANSFERENCE

The teacher can be experienced by the student as a cold, rejecting individual or a warm, caring person. The psychodynamic definition for the displacement of feelings about a person from the individual's past onto another person in the present is called transference. Transference is a powerful way the mind remembers the past, but does so indirectly through present relationships. In the teacher–student relationship, thoughts and feelings about someone from the student's past become emotionally activated and transferred onto another person in the student's present situation. In everyday life, we frequently observe a form of transference when we say, "My friend Alice reminds me of Aunt Ellen." Alice evokes memories, thoughts, and feelings about Aunt Ellen, who may have been experienced as supportive or critical. It is a concept teachers can use to understand and talk about stage fright. There are many "Aunt Ellens" in one's imaginary audience.

Transference may be considered a Letter B response of the student's regard for the teacher or the audience who is perceived, collectively, as parents or as significant others. The teacher is experienced both as she "is" in reality and also through the lens of the student's early relationships with meaningful others such as parents or siblings.

It is not surprising for some students to experience helpful instruction and suggestions by the teacher as criticism rather than support, if the student has had experiences that contributed to feeling criticized in the past (or were perceived as being criticized.) Perceptions are as meaningful psychologically as are scientifically verifiable events. Often the mind does not and cannot distinguish between what is "real" and what is "believed to be real." This, too, is transference. Some students may expect punishment or rejection from authority figures, particularly if there have been experiences with rejection, separation, loss, neglect, intimidation, pressure to be "perfect," or abuse in early years. This is transference. Each student will experience the teacher complexly and differently in the transference, often regardless of how the teacher acts in "reality."

One student can be quite fearful of hearing all teacher comments as criticisms and may try very hard to please. Another student may have low self-esteem and worry about not being good enough for a teacher to offer any compliments at all. Another student may appear defiant and sloppy in lesson preparation to silently suggest, "I don't care what you think." Another will feel very competitive with other students in the studio and try to be a favorite pupil. None of these situations automatically indicates a major mental disorder or reality about the teacher, but they illustrate a range of normal emotional reactions to reliving a past relationship in a present interaction with the teacher—in the transference. If the transference is persistent and interfering with the student/teacher relationship, the teacher can observe (not analyze) the student's silence, fearfulness, trying extraordinarily hard to be "right."

In performance, the audience, with its ability to applaud or reject the performer also can represent (through the psychodynamic concepts of transference and displacement) the parents and/or the music teacher. Performers wish to please the audience and to receive applause (emotional nourishment—originally experienced or not experienced in the nursery). Infancy is a time in life when children are totally dependent and parents *literally* are necessary for emotional and physical survival. The earliest interactions that occur, or do not occur, between parent and child often come alive emotionally in the studio and particularly on stage, when the student is under the pressures and challenges of performing. While performing can be intrinsically satisfying, it is also an interaction with others from whom the performer wants approval, appreciation, and applause. In this form of transference, the audience is "family." The audience and performer form a complex relationship with each other.

SHAME

Powerful emotions are at the root of performance anxiety, including the painful affects of shame, humiliation, and embarrassment. Students, and all people, dread feeling incompetent, inadequate, and looking foolish in front of others. Students are afraid of being laughed at for mistakes or mocked and bullied for being nervous. People who do not understand the depth and angst of performance anxiety will often, with good intentions, try to reassure or talk students out of feeling anxiety while encouraging them with rational ideas. Students may be reminded that they are prepared, talented, smart people, and advised that they should not be worried. This advice may help to a point. It may not.

Good preparation and proper repertoire are essential; there is no psychological theory or musical technique that will relieve performance anxiety without thorough musical and technical preparation. Simply practicing for longer hours or being reassured is not a solution for the complexity of anxiety, which can undermine the best-prepared, smartest, and most talented performers. *Performance anxiety is not only a musical problem.*

Realizing that performance anxiety is much more than skin deep, and that strong emotion can override rationality and preparation, teacher advice and reassurance can fall on frightened, not deaf, ears. Students, like all people, want to be understood, or at least feel that someone is trying to understand them. Students want to know that their feelings are taken seriously, that they are listened to, and that they will not be mocked or shamed for worrying.

Shame is both a feeling that one is inadequate, which is an emotion in the mind, *and* a fear that other people will mock or laugh at them, which is a social construct that occurs between people. Shame is a potent psychological and social issue that permeates the experience of performance anxiety. Although origins of shame begin early in life, shame has a long shelf-life. Teachers must be alerted to and acutely aware of this dynamic and the defenses students use to try to hide shame. It is often considered shameful to admit to feeling this "forbidden" emotion. We return to the important topic of shame in chapter 7.

It is difficult or impossible to console a highly anxious and fearful student with rationality. The student's observable behavior is not the entire story behind stage fright, although manifest anxiety always is important to note with empathy. While teachers should let the anxious student know that the teacher is trying to understand the student's feelings about shame, teachers must not become armchair psychotherapists to their students any more than a psychologist should try to be a music teacher to their musician patients. While many students do not need psychotherapy (although some students and teachers would benefit from exploring their emotional lives), the main points emphasized here are that appreciation of the complexity of the unconscious mind and awareness of the richness and depth of mental life are important attitudes for teachers to adopt in order to establish an atmosphere of openness and safety. Such attitudes permit trust and foster listening and learning in the intimate one-to-one relationship that develops in the teaching studio.

COUNTERTRANSFERENCE

The challenges of working with anxious students can raise feelings of confusion, worry, insecurity, annoyance, anxiety, helplessness, and anger in teachers. Teachers may be sharing affects that are similar to those the student is experiencing. Provocative, needy, forgetful, angry, or anxious people tend to evoke similar affects in others. So, too, do ingratiating and chronically "too sweet" people. The nature of personal interactions in the studio gives rise automatically to transference (student's subjective feelings toward teacher), but also evokes the teacher's subjective reaction toward the student.

Countertransference, like transference, is a Letter B emotional response of the teacher toward the student. Naturally, teachers develop feelings toward those with whom they work. Teachers are not blank slates, nor should they be. Awareness of one's emotions can be informative, should not be dismissed, and can be used for reflection and as problem-solving mental "tools" in teaching. The teacher must become aware of any strong emotional reaction toward the student, which could be annoyance and/or favoritism, and endeavor to keep the relationship in the studio both genuine and professional. Otherwise, the teacher will be inclined to act in ways that are unprofessional such as giving extra time routinely, offering highly critical praise, making sarcastic comments to students, being chronically late or canceling lessons, and/or making special arrangements for some students and not others. Actions and attitudes of teachers, communicated silently without a word spoken to others, also may interfere with professional boundaries. Judgment often is influenced by emotional responses. It will help immensely for teachers to talk with other teachers or a mental health professional should the teacher realize that personal feelings are impeding the teacher–student relationship. In the worst scenario, inappropriate boundary crossing can occur, which is highly damaging to both student and teacher. It is imperative for teachers to have a balanced and rewarding life outside the teaching studio to be most effective in their professional roles.

MULTIPLE FUNCTION

The concept of multiple function suggests that, similar to an enharmonic note that has two names (e.g., D flat and C sharp), or a chord that can function both as a dominant and tonic tonality, there are multiple meanings for any emotional reaction or behavior. One example of mental multiple function is that the teacher and audience unconsciously can represent a "good, loving parent" *and* an "angry and disapproving" parent. Mental life is complex, continually dynamic (changing, evolving), and full of contradictions and paradoxes. One's psychological history and one's subjective interpretation of life events accompanies students at lessons and on stage in every performance. Playing in public involves more than playing all the right notes. In the psychodynamic model of mental life, what we hear people say on the surface is only a part of a broad, multilayered, deeply personal story. Teachers can help students with performance anxiety by being careful listeners and observers of words, behaviors, and feelings while appreciating that the whole student (and teacher) is more than the sum of his or her psychological parts.

Vignette: Joe

Joe, age twelve, was going to perform in a music festival. He practiced carefully and knew his music. His teacher arranged a number of tryouts for him so he could practice playing repertoire in front of others before the big day. While Joe felt nervous in these situations, he performed well and his anxiety was manageable. However, as the festival got closer, Joe became increasingly anxious. He did not talk about it, but started to leave his music at home, made unusual mistakes in his pieces, and began to act sullen at his lessons (symptoms).

Joe's teacher knew that her student had a number of challenges as a toddler, including an illness that required hospitalization for a week during which Joe was separated from his parents much of the time. Joe underwent painful treatment, and he felt he had no control. Although he recovered, Joe became suspicious of authority figures, such as doctors (and teachers) who were supposed to help him but whom Joe feared would hurt him (transference). His teacher began to think that Joe was fearful of the judges at the festival, and that he worried about being "perfect." In other words, Joe had transposed the fear of being "ill" to the fear of not being "perfect" in performing. Joe's toddler experience came alive years later when he felt anxious.

Joe's teacher understood that his unusual and sudden behavior was a nonverbal communication that Joe was telling her "something"—that perhaps she had become, through Joe's unconscious transference to her, an unreliable adult. She talked with him about his fears about performing and his changes in behavior that she observed at lessons. She did not offer an interpretation, but did think privately to herself about some psychological implications of the medical history she understood about Joe.

Joe welcomed his teacher's interest and gradually began to talk with her about his performance anxiety. He did not realize that he was transferring childhood feelings onto his teacher, and she did not mention her suspicion of this to him. Just talking with Joe opened up his mental pathways to feel better about the festival and not view it as a time when he was a helpless child and reliant on decisions of doctors (and music judges). Joe subsequently felt more in control of himself playing his instrument.

Joe approached the festival with greater self-confidence and played well. Joe's teacher did not react toward his atypical behavior in a negative or angry way (countertransference), nor did she try to become his psychologist (she maintained professional boundaries). The teacher became curious about Joe and opened pathways for understanding and communication.

The teacher had developed a form that parents filled out with information regarding developmental milestones and health information about previous injury and illness, so she was informed about some of Joe's past without asking him personal questions about his health history. She used this information confidentially and privately in order to better understand Joe. Joe's teacher added her understanding of symptoms, transference and countertransference to her teaching toolbox.

PSYCHOLOGICAL AND PRACTICAL TIPS

When understanding the complex psychological processes that occur consciously and unconsciously through the concepts of transference and countertransference, the teacher can encourage and foster greater psychological security within students while also sharing practical help to increase their performance security. Teachers, as positive transferential figures, can help students use their own mind so that both mental and music security and self-esteem will be enhanced.

The following activity will lead to helpful discussions. The following ideas can be useful both in private lessons and in groups.

Activity: Imagine This

- Imagine yourself practicing for your recital at home.
- Imagine seeing the music on the page.
- Imagine yourself getting ready to go to the recital.
- Imagine what you are wearing (including shoes—important for pedaling and comfort walking on and off stage).
- Imagine eating a healthy snack before you go to the recital.
- Imagine arriving at the recital venue.
- Imagine seeing other students coming in.
- Imagine that you are next on the program.
- Imagine walking on stage.
- Imagine bowing.
- Imagine starting the first piece.
- Imagine you are anxious but you use a Letter B tip to deal with your anxiety.
- Imagine bowing after you finish.
- Imagine feeling good about your performance.

Teachers and students can create additional recital images of their own. Continue discussing each image until the student can truly visualize it, speak about it, and begin to feel greater comfort in managing feelings about the recital. If students do not want to talk about themselves, teachers can use a fictional character or a famous person as the "model" performer who replies to the questions.

IMPLICATIONS FOR TEACHERS

- Teachers need to be aware of the importance of infancy and early childhood in mental life, since developmental issues are embedded in performance anxiety.
- Teachers must be aware that symptoms are unique ways students express anxiety.
- Teachers should realize that performing can revive early experiences around approval, appreciation, and fears of rejection in students.
- Teachers should appreciate that performance anxiety originates off stage and is triggered by anticipating or giving a performance.
- Teachers should appreciate the concepts of transference and countertransference since these psychological dynamics are alive inside (and outside) the studio.
- Teachers should discuss and normalize the affect of shame with students when students express self-doubts and anxiety about looking foolish or stupid.
- Teachers need to be aware that most of mental life is unconscious and outside of conscious awareness.
- Teachers must be aware of keeping boundaries and of maintaining a professional, genuine atmosphere both in and outside the studio.
- Teachers must create a private life outside their studio.

7

DEFENDING AGAINST ANXIETY

QUESTIONS FOR THOUGHT

- What is an ego defense?
- Why does the mind defend itself against anxiety?
- What are some adaptive and maladaptive ways the mind defends against anxiety?
- List some ego defenses that may be used by students.
- Identify ego defenses as Letter B responses.

PERFORMANCE AS A DANGER SITUATION: EGO DEFENSES

The human mind is very creative, and it *defends* itself against real or perceived dangers and threats. Performance is experienced as an emotional danger and threat to the performer's competence and self-esteem. How one approaches or avoids a threat is important, as dealing with threats can be adaptive or maladaptive. A defense in itself is neither good nor bad. A defense is a Letter B response, which has been introduced in earlier chapters and referred to as symptoms and conflicts. A psychological defense against a perceived or real danger is a subjective feeling, behavior, or thought. Psychological defenses against anxiety are called ego defenses because the mind is protecting itself from the threat of anxiety.

THE EGO AND ITS DEFENSES AGAINST ANXIETY

The *ego* is part of the psychological organization of the mind, a source of energy, and it serves as a mental buffer zone between the conscious (thoughts and feelings of which one is *aware*) and the unconscious (thoughts and feelings of which one is *unaware*). The ego is also the mental mediator/referee between one's external and internal life, between the uninhibited internal forces of the unconscious *id* and the ethics, propriety, and morality of the *superego* functions of the mind. The ego is an important "moderator" of feelings, behavior, and self-concept. The ego is not a part of one's biological anatomy. The ego's primary function is to provide emotional adaptation (ego defenses) both to the outside world and to cope with thoughts and feelings that live deep inside the mind.

As an example in everyday life, when people know that weighing too much (Letter A) may lead to high blood pressure and other health hazards (Letter C), people typically "defend" (take care of) themselves with diet, exercise, and, at times, with medication (Letter B). However, some people do not take the steps necessary to ward off illness. Some people put risk aside, or think "I'll get around to this at another time," or convince themselves, "I'm not going to get sick. I feel fine now" (Letter B). When an underlying physical or emotional condition is not acknowledged seriously and dealt with appropriately, it will be repeated, and unfortunate consequences may be experienced.

For the performer, an approaching recital could be experienced as both a "danger" and an exciting experience and, ideally, would lead to careful practice. An impending recital could also make many performers very nervous. Some people would prepare carefully (adaptive ego defense). Others may think that hard work is not necessary because "things usually turn out all right" (maladaptive ego defense). Sometimes things do turn out all right. Luck can be mercurial. To put something "scary" out of one's mind does not make it go away. This form of denial (an ego defense) actually increases the probability that the recital or audition will not turn out all right.

If ego defenses (Table 7.1) are not helpful (Letter B) and anxiety remains unconscious, the student will likely experience various debilitating symptoms (Letter B) instead of relief (a function of adaptive ego defenses at Letter B). In such

Table 7.1

TYPICAL EGO DEFENSES (MALADAPTIVE/ ADAPTIVE DEPENDING ON HOW USED BY INDIVIDUALS)

(A definition and unhelpful/helpful examples are illustrated)

Projection: What you think others think about you.
The audience will not/will like me.

Rationalization: Use common sense to minimize anxiety.
It is ok not to practice today/I need to practice to be ready for my lesson.

Denial: Believing something or someone does not exist.
I do not feel anxious/I feel anxious so I better practice.

Reaction Formation: Saying the opposite of what you feel.
Nothing bothers me about performing/Performing is hard.

Isolation of Affect: Showing little emotion when anxious.
No problem, I'm doing fine/I'm freaked out and I am scared.

Note: Any thought, feeling, or behavior can be used as an adaptive or maladaptive (helpful or unhelpful) ego defense. Defenses are typically used in combination, since mental life is complex.

cases where there are maladaptive ego defenses, anxiety will persist or escalate. The following vignette explains how ego defenses worked (or did not work) for Mary. Table 7.1 illustrates examples of adaptive and maladaptive ego defenses. Table 7.2 lists emotions, thoughts, and bodily symptoms of performance anxiety that can function as ego defenses.

Vignette: Mary

With her senior recital approaching in a couple of months, Mary started dating a guy she liked a lot. Mary spent hours on the phone talking with him. She told herself, " I will get to my practicing later," but she became enchanted with her new boyfriend's attention. "Later" never seemed to happen.

Mary stayed up late texting with her boyfriend, so she could not get up early and practice before school. She managed to accomplish a minimum amount of work through "panic" practice a few days prior to her recital, but she felt very shaky when she walked on stage. Her preparation had been compromised by her longing for attention from her boyfriend. Mary feared if she was not available to be with him he would find another girlfriend.

Mary's situation is not different from that of many other adolescents. Teenagers have boyfriends, extracurricular activities, homework, athletic activities, and enormous pulls on their time, energy, and self-esteem. The results of such conflicts may become evident in the teaching studio and observed in how students prepare for lessons and recitals.

Teachers have the opportunity and responsibility to listen to how students talk about their feelings (Letter B—which now can be understood as symptoms, conflicts, and ego defenses), and teachers can help students develop constructive ways to practice and to better manage their time. Defining and talking about ego defenses with students in studio classes and in private lessons helps empower students to find ways to balance their busy lives and feelings and to perform with greater confidence. While it is not appropriate for teachers to analyze students' ego defenses, teachers can be tuned into students' symptoms and ego defenses from a psychological viewpoint (Table 7.2). This understanding leads to better communication in the studio

Table 7.2

PERFORMANCE ANXIETY SYMPTOMS AS EGO DEFENSES (LETTER B)

Psychological (Emotions/Feelings)	Physical (Body)
I feel embarrassed	My hands are shaking
I fear humiliation	My heart is beating fast
I feel helpless	My hands are sweating
I worry about audience reaction	My stomach hurts
I feel self-consciousness	My chest is tight
I am afraid of technique not working	I cannot sleep
I worry about memory slips	My hands are cold
Cognitions (Thoughts)	
I will not play well	
My teacher/friends will not like me	
I know what they are thinking	
I look stupid	
I will mess up	
I will be ashamed	
People will laugh at me	
I do not want to be in another recital	
I want to stop lessons	

Note: These lists of psychological, physical, and cognitive examples are not listed in any particular order. There are no correlations implied among the three lists, nor does one list equate with another. The objective is to illustrate that there are multiple mental processes that may occur simultaneously regarding ego defenses, conflicts, and symptoms. The mind and body are intimately interdependent in mental life.

and informed pedagogy that emphasizes both musical competence and mental health.

Letter B

An illustrative list of Mary's ego defenses (Letter B) is offered below. A definition is provided after each ego defense and is followed by a general example of an unhelpful use of that defense. Following the general example, an example is offered to illustrate how Mary used each ego defense (Letter B). Note that Mary's ego defenses were not adaptive or helpful as she approached (and avoided) her performance preparation, and it is likely she will experience heightened stage fright.

> PROJECTION: The belief that other people are thinking something (usually uncomplimentary) about you.
> GENERAL EXAMPLE: If I have a memory slip, the audience will not like me.
> MARY: If I am not always able to see my boyfriend he will not like me and will date someone else.

> RATIONALIZATION: An attempt to minimize or explain away a thought or feeling, typically using common sense.
> GENERAL EXAMPLE: I was late to school because I had to make my lunch.
> MARY: I will practice tomorrow because I already know the music.

> DENIAL: Believing that something does not exist.
> GENERAL EXAMPLE: I bet my teacher won't choose me to play in the recital.

MARY: I will not worry about this recital because it is so far in the future.

REACTION FORMATION: Saying or feeling the *opposite* of what one really thinks or feels.
GENERAL EXAMPLE: I don't know why everyone else freaks out about performing. I am pretty relaxed about it.
MARY: I am not nervous at all about this recital.

ISOLATION OF AFFECT: The inability to experience or acknowledge feelings so that one talks about a highly charged topic with little or no emotion.
GENERAL EXAMPLE: I had a memory slip in the last recital but that does not bother me.
MARY: I really do not care about what the audience thinks.

The ego defenses (or unconscious "excuses") Mary used perhaps helped ward off her performance anxiety temporarily, but they did not help her prepare for the recital or avoid last-minute panic. They were unhelpful in the long-term. She probably did not realize the consequences of what she was thinking and feeling about performing versus being with her boyfriend. Common sense, cajoling, reasoning, or being rational probably would not have made a difference to Mary. It could have been helpful for her teacher to address her ego defenses and emphasize that procrastinating with her practice (another ego defense) would not be in her best interest with a recital on the horizon. The teacher could offer Mary alternative ways to defend herself against her performance anxiety with time management that could allow both for practice and time for boyfriend.

Mary unknowingly (unconsciously) was struggling with self-esteem issues, which were particularly challenged when she felt anxious. Her new boyfriend boosted her self-esteem. Her responses (ego defenses) to the impending recital reflected her attempts to distance herself emotionally from her anxiety instead of using an effective coping tool kit to defend adaptively to her inner fears of "danger" about performing.

A constructive way teachers can help students cope with low self-esteem and worry about what the boyfriend, aka "audience," thinks (which typically is a *projection* of what students think about themselves) is to recognize how students talk about (or avoid talking about) recitals and feelings. When negative, avoidant, and self-deprecating statements (Letter B) are recognized by the teacher, the teacher can offer new ways to adaptively approach the anxiety "danger" that the student fears.

A B C MODEL OF ANXIETY

The A B C Model of Anxiety will be discussed more fully so that teachers and students will recognize how Letter B fits into an overall understanding of how the ego defends against anxiety. This model also identifies possible consequences represented by Letter C of various ego defenses employed at Letter B.

Activity 1—Recognizing Anxiety

Recognizing Ego Defenses in the ABC Model
A B C

A = Performance
B = Thoughts, feelings, physical reactions (ego defenses)[1]
C = Consequences (how one performs; self-esteem)

Recognizing Anxiety

1. Think of a stressful performance (letter A)

2. What did you say, think, feel about the stressful performance? (Letter B)

Discuss with your teacher or make a list of your thoughts, feelings, and body sensations (Letter B).

3. Rate your anxiety (performance "temperature"/Arc of Anxiety)

1 . . . . 2 . . . . 3 . . . . 4 . . . . 5 . . . . 6 . . . . 7 . . . . 8 . . . . 9 10
low anxiety   high anxiety

4. List some ego defenses that you used (Letter B).
    1.
    2.
    3.

5. Did you use helpful or unhelpful ego defenses?
    1.
    2.
    3.

---

[1] Teachers should keep in mind that *symptoms* and *conflicts* discussed in previous chapters are *ego defenses.*

Activity 2—Relabeling Anxiety

Rethinking Ego Defenses and the A B C Model

1. Think of a stressful performance (Letter A)

2. What did you say, think, feel about the stressful performance? (Letter B)

3. Rate your anxiety (performance "temperature"/Arc of Anxiety)

1 .... 2 .... 3 .... 4 .... 5 .... 6 .... 7 .... 8 .... 9 10
low anxiety   high anxiety

4. Challenge any unhelpful responses Letter B (unhelpful ego defenses)

    1.

    2.

    3.

5. Relabel Letter B (adaptive ego defenses)

6. Rerate your anxiety

1 .... 2 .... 3 .... 4 .... 5 .... 6 .... 7 .... 8 .... 9 10
low anxiety   high anxiety

7. List some of the adaptive ego defenses you used

    1.

    2.

    3.

8. Were your adaptive ego defenses helpful in lowering anxiety?

Suggestions for Adaptive/Helpful Ego Defenses
(Self-Statements) to Enhance Self-Esteem and Lower
Performance Anxiety

- I cannot make everyone appreciate me, no matter how I perform.
- I will do the best I can. I practiced carefully, and I am prepared.
- I will focus on what I am doing, not on what people may think.
- If I do not think highly of myself, it is likely I will project that same feeling onto others and believe they do not like me.
- Mistakes do not make me a terrible person. I am *sharing* the music with others—I do not have to *prove* anything.
- It doesn't help me to compare myself with anyone else; we all are different. Thank goodness for that!

As emphasized, performance anxiety, which is experienced as a "danger," rests to a great extent on one's self-evaluation and self-statements. One can be one's own worst critic, but also one's own best supporter. An adaptive use of ego defenses helps the performer appreciate one's talent, enjoy one's realistic abilities, and prepare steadily and conscientiously. If one is anxious, it is helpful to admit it and deal with anxiety constructively. Feelings that are buried stay in one's mental underground and are far away from conscious awareness. Buried feelings will not go away on their own.

If performance makes students highly anxious, students will resort to typical old ways of defending themselves. Even though old ways may not be helpful, they are familiar. For example, if a student rationalizes that one can practice later, the student is not directly facing anxiety about the approaching recital and the necessity to practice consistently. (Avoidance and procrastination are also ego defenses—Letter B.) The recital date and anxiety will not disappear. Mary avoided and procrastinated practicing. It did not help her. Ironically, one can think of stage fright itself as an ego defense to avoid confronting more painful feelings, fears, and memories.

We return to Cindy, whom we met earlier, as another way to further illustrate ego defenses (Letter B). Teachers can use this story as a creative stimulus for the activities on ego defenses.

Vignette: Cindy's Cold Hands as Ego Defenses

As you recall, Cindy suffered with cold hands, which was the way her body physically "spoke" about her anxiety. She also feared her teacher would not like her playing at lessons, and she was frequently inhibited in her musical expression of original ideas. Therefore, we can say she projected *her anxiety about her own perceived inadequacy onto her convictions about teacher's opinion of her, making the teacher the one who disapproved of Cindy. Yet, Cindy knew that on one level, it was she who was worried about herself, as her teacher never gave indication that she was unhappy with her student. Here we also see an example of* rationalization, *since Cindy knew on an intellectual level her teacher was her ally. Also, on some level, Cindy knew it was not the cold room that was responsible for her anxiety, but unconsciously, she rationalized that it was because the affects around coldness (around her parents' divorce and mother's depression) were too painful to understand consciously. These painful feelings were deeply connected to her childhood issues of profound sadness, loss, and her presumption of guilt. Cindy was unable to think of this connection on her own and could only focus on her symptoms. Because Cindy's parents had indeed been good parents and had never realized how their own problems affected their daughter, Cindy* denied *that their divorce and her loss of her childhood home had anything to do with her performance anxiety when she became a young adult. The divorce had been years ago! Because Cindy had a good enough relationship with her mother and loved her very much, she could not realize that she also harbored anger toward her mother's moodiness. Thus, Cindy's* reaction formation *of always being the good, dependable girl and talented student covered her angry feelings. After all, she had always believed that anger caused people to leave and separate, so she had to* isolate her affects *(angry feelings) when they surfaced. Instead, she found herself anxious at lessons and on stage.*

SHAME MASQUERADING AS A RESISTANCE TO PERFORMANCE

The powerful affect of shame and its early emergence emotionally in the life cycle begs further discussion as it pertains to performance anxiety. Shame can be both an ego defense expressed as an affect (e.g., "I am a*nxious* about messing up my performance in front of my peers and my teacher") and/or an action and reaction from others (e.g., "I will make many mistakes in public and my friends will laugh at me"). Shame also rears its fearsome head in the student/teacher relationship in the guise of forgetting lesson times or repeatedly canceling lessons, not paying the teacher's bill, and/or losing music. In such cases, the student is fearful of feeling ashamed about himself when he plays his instrument, so various ego defenses are used unconsciously to ward off what is feared the most, feeling small, vulnerable, and incompetent. When chronic, these ego defenses and behaviors, motivated by shame and anxiety, can create frustration and annoyance for the teacher who is attempting to be helpful, but who becomes increasingly puzzled. They can introduce a wedge in the teacher–student relationship that results in very knotty teaching and performance issues.

The music lesson is a performance by the student for the teacher, with the teacher being perceived as an "audience" and a projected (potentially) critical parent-substitute. Many of the overt feelings and behaviors about appearing on stage also come alive in the music lesson and in the teacher/student relationship. This includes shame.

SHAME ON YOU!

The psychodynamics of earliest childhood underlie the evolution of shame responses. This is particularly relevant for musicians because there may be (1) an early age of involvement with a musical instrument and (2) subsequent difficulties later in life in finding and sustaining career opportunities in one's chosen profession, should the young music student turn professional. Specifically pertinent are fears about rejection, loss, and competition that take root in earliest childhood and may intensify as one grows up. Emphasized here is the central idea that artistic and personal identity coalesce and share parallel psychic and artistic pathways over one's life span.

Melodies in the nursery involve not only emotional nourishment and care of bodily needs but also attention paid to the nonverbal communication between mother and child. Mother responds to baby's gurgles and coos as the pair engages in their first musical duets. With good-enough (not perfect) parenting, these nonspoken interactions are consonant. Sometimes this music is dissonant. Earliest sounds, silences, and impressions between parents and children form the foundation for a sense of security and self-esteem that, depending on how they are internalized by the child, can reappear years later in the emergence of stage fright.

The performer/audience relationship offers musicians the opportunity to express wishes, hopes, anxieties, and fantasies of rewards and fears from the public, experienced as parents, through the ego defenses of projection and displacement. Perceived "good" and "bad" audiences rekindle affects and physical sensations from earliest relationships. For those musicians who have chronic and performance-threatening stage fright, their earliest "bad review" (or perceived "bad review") potentially came from those on whom their debut performance depended most, namely, their caregivers. At a tender age, the evolving sense of having an impact on and trusting others—and trusting oneself—is formative and internalized deep inside the mind. Thus, the seeds of performance anxiety can begin as early as infancy.

For the older child, adolescent, and adult musician, talent and performance ability can become tangled in a fantasy of controlling a mother or significant other, represented in displacement by the teacher. For the highly anxious performer, pleasure in one's skill and realistic accomplishments are neither trusted nor enjoyed intrinsically. Since the performer may have little confidence in his ability to trust or have a desired effect on another from his earliest years, he falls back on a magical belief that he must *coerce* the audience/parent/teacher to love him. The highly anxious performer may employ "magic thinking," (that is, an emphasis on perfect technique, brilliant interpretations) to command the desired response from the (m)other. These affects cast a powerful shadow over all performance situations.

It is not a big leap to realize that for performance anxious musicians, a fragile self is on the firing line every time they appear on stage. For performers who measure self-love primarily from external sources, positive self-regard is predominantly obtained through teacher approval and audience applause. There is difficulty in believing in one's intrinsic self-worth without the roar of the crowd, which hinges on some performers' beliefs that they can control the crowd through a brilliant, sensitive, and technically "perfect" performance. Such performers typically feel depressed—sometimes ill—if they cannot achieve this goal. Pleasure in one's competence is absent in the pursuit of magic and omnipotence.

Verbal expressions often reveal the shame that can fuel performance anxiety. For example, descriptions of musical insecurities often are metaphors for bodily insecurities about dreaded structural and functional defects, which include malfunctions of memory and technique when playing a musical instrument. The prototype of normal early childhood narcissistic exhibitionistic exuberance—showing off and hamming it up—becomes tangled in an affective and defensive web of shame at being viewed negatively in public and fear of being laughed at by others. Residues of childhood fascination with how bodies work—or don't—are heard in performers' potty talk expressions such as making "boo boos," "having accidents," "making a mess" and "dropping notes." Fear of emotional and musical incontinence in public becomes unconsciously associated with the dreaded loss of bodily control (i.e., the embarrassing loss of musical technique and memory slips, the symptoms that frequently bring performers to psychological treatment). Shame on those performers who make a mess on stage! Who would want to feel naked, to appear small, and to be ridiculed in front of an audience?

A FUSION OF MUSICAL
AND PERSONAL IDENTITY

The confluence of musical and personal identity are fused for many musicians. Excerpts from an article by Janet Horvath in *The Atlantic* are quoted below (Horvath, 2015). Ms. Horvath poignantly illustrates how her music career and her personal identity were significantly challenged when her career had to be reconsidered and redirected.

Ms. Horvath experienced an auditory injury, hyperacusis, that made her unable to tolerate sound. What could be worse for a musician? The implications of her condition pointed to the end of an orchestral career that spanned over 30 years.

> The doctor told me gently, but prolonged exposure (to sound) would only make things worse. It would be best if I left my job and did something else, something quiet. . . . I knew I wouldn't listen. Giving up a 34-year career was unthinkable; playing cello was at the core of my identity.

Deciding to ignore medical advice, she ventured on a European tour. Her pain was intolerable, particularly when performing the Beethoven 9th Symphony that included a 250-member chorus.

> When we returned to the U.S., I made an appointment with the maestro and the upper management of the Minnesota

Orchestra and resigned my position of 31 years as associate-principal cello. Unable to face my colleagues, I left them a note with my goodbyes, returned to my cloistered existence, and promptly sunk into a deep depression. . . . For months, getting out of bed was a feat of willpower. Taunted by a closet full of elegant black clothing, the uniform of orchestra members, I donated it all to Goodwill. My cello sat unused in its case, a reminder of what I'd lost. My normally animated personality changed as I became subdued and soft-spoken. I spent a lot of time wondering how athletes deal with career-ending injuries, about how they rebuild their lives after being carried off the field for the last time on a stretcher. My own sense of identity crumbled. . . . It was excruciating that what I loved so much could bring me so much pain.

Ms. Horvath finally found a specialist who helped her, although she was not able to return to orchestral playing.

I can comfortably play with three or four other musicians in a modest-sized room. It's not an orchestra, but it's enough. Life is unthinkable without music.

She does not mention whether she sought psychological help to deal with her shame and loss, which could have assisted in her transition.

HELPING STUDENTS DISCOVER THEIR EGO DEFENSES

When teachers start conceptualizing music lessons as performances in the studio, consider themselves as an audience, and understand that shame is a devastating emotion that masks the ego defense of "resistance" for students, they are in a better position to deal constructively with what is often pejoratively referred to as a "resistant or noncooperative" student. Teachers also will begin to recognize the "too eager to please student" is a form of resistance, as the student tries hard to impress before she feels shamed with feeling inadequate. Both avoidant students and those who are "too eager to please the teacher" may be struggling with performance anxiety. When teachers understand that students are not being defiant, bad, disinterested, or too eager, they will automatically handle the student's shame-fueled performance anxiety (often masked as avoidance) in a more productive and compassionate manner.

Teachers can help students discover and identify ego defenses (Letter B) and discuss whether their ego defenses are helpful and lower anxiety or unhelpful and raise anxiety. Students can work toward developing greater conscious awareness about their anxiety and use adaptive ego defenses (which they may start to call "Letter B" as a familiar verbal shortcut). This kind of instruction can help students adapt more comfortably to their feelings and to a performance situation. Teachers can help students feel better about themselves and their performing by talking about performance feelings in every lesson and studio class. While this may sound easy, it is the most challenging part of assisting students both to own and to handle their performance anxiety. To recognize how one is contributing to one's own stage fright takes courage, persistence, and perseverance. The effort is worth it both for teachers and students.

Teachers can spark students to see something in themselves about which students have been afraid and unaware. By adding performance anxiety strategies to teaching strategies, teachers assist students with their mental health and emotional development in a manner that is profoundly psychodynamic, growth promoting, and infinitely rewarding.

Dealing successfully with performance anxiety is not about deceiving oneself, denying fears, and simply replacing them with "positive self-talk." This does not work in the long run—or short run!! Teachers can help students take an honest and serious inventory of all feelings and thoughts about stage fright. Performance anxiety is complex, painful, and normal because it reflects the richness, depth, and uniqueness of each person's mind.

IMPLICATIONS FOR TEACHERS

- It is important for the teacher to be genuinely empathetic, to avoid becoming judgmental, and to adopt an attitude of curiosity and willingness to talk about all student feelings and behaviors. This attitude will invite the student to model the teacher's attitude and reflect on behavior and feelings.
- Teachers can instill hope that students can overcome learning difficulties and musical and emotional setbacks.
- The teacher can encourage the student to think, reflect, and develop problem-solving skills in addition to music technique.
- Teachers must foster an atmosphere of safety, comfort, and respect in the studio. Students will realize that mistakes or chronically forgetting to practice are symptoms, not "bad, defiant behavior." These symptoms or ego defenses can be explored in order to understand some underlying reasons that lead to mistakes and forgetfulness.

- Teachers can augment their own understanding of student "avoidance behaviors" as examples of student fears and defenses to ward-off (avoid) shame, humiliation, and embarrassment.
- Teachers must offer assistance to solve musical, not personal problems. The teacher will promote tolerance, curiosity, and new attitudes about understanding student fears, leading to a healthy atmosphere in the studio.
- Teachers will reinforce the idea that mistakes are not "bad" but provide learning opportunities. Development of curious attitudes (vs. disapproval) about mistakes make a difference in self-esteem, which enhances pleasure in music making.
- Teachers must discuss the wish for "perfection" with students (and often with parents) and emphasize that sharing music, not striving for "perfection," is the desired goal.
- Teachers lay the groundwork to appreciate that in reality things can turn out "OK" when everyone, including the performer, is not "perfect."
- Teachers will recognize that some children have come to expect and fear, with or without reason, that parents and teachers demand "perfection." One does not need to seek the illusion of being "perfect" to receive parental or others' love and attention.
- Teachers will benefit from understanding the concepts of transference and countertransference. The private studio, with its one-to-one relationship, uniquely fosters these attitudes from both teachers and students.

- Teachers will benefit from realizing that student (and teacher) behavior and feelings often are unconscious. This realization allows the teacher to understand problematic situations in a way that allows for increased patience, and to develop an attitude that appreciates that the student is communicating a message expressed in "action language."

- Teachers can realize that the way students react with the teacher is a variation of how students have interacted with other important authority figures, including parents and significant others. The realization that the student is *transferring* (transference) old feelings onto a "new" person, the teacher, allows teachers to understand behaviors that appear to be thwarting the learning process. This realization enhances the teacher's ability to evenly, and not defensively, approach difficult issues that arise at lessons.

- Teachers will have reactions toward their pupils' attitudes and behaviors (*countertransference*—or counter feelings). When the teacher realizes that a student has become a "favorite" or "problem" student, the teacher is in a position to reflect privately on his or her own personal attitudes and early relationships that may have given rise to such reactions.

- Teachers can consider the concept of *multiple function* to better understand the multiple complexities, inconsistencies, and paradoxes in students and in themselves. Students can be motivated *and* resistant at the same time. The teacher can then use some of the tools in the mental tool kit to address conflict, symptoms, and ego defenses.

8

LEARNING THEORY AND

BEHAVIOR MODIFICATION

QUESTIONS FOR THOUGHT

- What is the difference between psychodynamic theory and behavioral theory?
- What is classical conditioning?
- What is operant conditioning?
- What are some ethical considerations about controlling behavior?
- How can teachers use behavioral techniques in the studio?

LEARNING THEORIES AS GUIDELINES FOR TEACHERS

Music teachers shape students' musical skills in a variety of ways. Teaching correct notes, fingering, phrasing, dynamics, and interpretive options are basic pedagogical tools. How these skills are taught fosters both a learning environment and a unique relationship between teacher and student. Music teachers intuitively use psychological techniques as they correct, encourage, reward, and offer alternative ways of learning and performing music. Teaching skills are represented in the field of psychology and are associated with learning theories, which emphasize concepts about conditioning and shaping behavior. This chapter discusses two basic learning theories. These are classical conditioning and operant conditioning. Cognitive behavior modification, as an outgrowth of classical and operant conditioning, will be presented in Chapter 9.

CLASSICAL CONDITIONING

In the 1900s in North America, some researchers and therapists in the mental health community became interested in the role of conscious experience, that is, thoughts about which one is consciously aware as well as behaviors that can be directly observed. The emergence of behaviorism occurred in this environment, with a focus on current behavior. Underlying unconscious motivation, as set forth by Sigmund Freud's (1856–1939) revolutionary theory and treatment called psychoanalysis is not a behavioral tenet, although psychoanalysts are acutely aware of "here and now" interactions in the consulting room as clues to underlying unconscious motivations. Fundamental behavioral theory and methodology for treatment differs from psychodynamic models. According to the behavioral model of the mind, both normal and abnormal behavior is *learned* through reinforcements and punishments, which are considered conditioning.

John Watson (1878–1958), an American psychologist, set the stage for behaviorism. Watson maintained that *learning* was achieved through connections and associations that the mind establishes when events occur simultaneously. This passage from Watson is often quoted:

> Give me a dozen healthy infants, well-formed, and my own specified world to bring them up in and I'll guarantee to take any one at random and train him to become any type of specialist I might select—doctor, lawyer, artist, merchant-chief, and, yes, even beggarman and thief, regardless of his talents, penchants, tendencies, abilities, vocations, and race of his ancestors. I am going beyond my facts and I admit it, but so have the advocates of the contrary and they have been doing it for many thousands of years.
>
> (WATSON, 1930, p. 82)

Strict behaviorists maintain that any behavior can be taught to any person through a process called conditioning. This technique, referred to as classical conditioning,[1] involves pairing a behavior with a neutral unconditioned stimulus. Gradually, the neutral stimulus evokes the unconditioned response as the mind begins to associate, or link, the two conditions together. Classical conditioning is associated with Ivan Pavlov (1849–1936), whose experiments involved hungry dogs who salivated at the sight of meat (unconditioned stimulus) that was paired with a bell (conditioned stimulus). After presenting the dogs with both the meat and the bell numerous times, the dogs would salivate when they heard only the bell (the meat was not present). The dogs' response to the bell became a *conditioned* response.

Orthodox behavioral theory maintains that moods and emotions (reflecting the invisible unconscious mind) are

[1] There are various methods of conditioning according to differing behavioral theories. I begin here with *classical* conditioning.

too subjective to be measured, and that only observable behaviors can be predicted, controlled, and measured. John Watson has become known for his famous experiment that created a phobia about white furry rats in Little Albert, a small boy under a year old. The experiment was conducted at Johns Hopkins University by Watson and his graduate student, Rosalie Rayner, and was published in 1920 in the *Journal of Experimental Psychology*. In his scientific protocol, Watson paired exposure of a furry rat with a scary noise, which created a rat phobia in a child who had not been afraid of little furry animals. Fears that are created according to this method of pairing can generalize to other furry objects, animals, and people, such as dogs, cats, and even men's beards.

Albert's phobia was created in a laboratory; he was never deconditioned, and sadly, Albert died from a rare illness by the time he was six years old. The ethics of this experiment, as well as immediate and far-ranging consequences and ethical considerations are brought into sharp focus with this approach to controlling, generalizing, and shaping behavior.

Teachers (and parents) greatly influence the behaviors of students and children in numerous overt and subtle ways. Performing in public becomes associated with fear and anxiety for many students. This fear can lead to dreaded memory and technical accidents. In the context of classical conditioning, performance anxiety would be labeled a conditioned response, where performing in public becomes conditioned to the affect of anxiety and the concrete stimulus of a stage and an audience. According to classical conditioning, performance anxiety can be deconditioned by pairing the stage with nonarousing stimuli. Techniques for extinguishing (or diminishing) performance anxiety are discussed later in this chapter. Letter B, which has been illustrated in earlier chapters, is used as a way to clarify how the teacher can use some conditioning psychological techniques in the studio.

OPERANT CONDITIONING

Another American psychologist who made an enormous early impact in the field of behaviorism was B.F. Skinner (1904–1990). Skinner suggested that rewards and punishments shape behavior. Skinner's model is known as operant conditioning. Skinner proposed that reinforced behaviors are strengthened and will be repeated; behavior that is not reinforced will be extinguished. Skinner identified three types of reinforcements that result in different behavioral consequences.

1. Neutral responses neither increase nor decrease a behavior.
2. Reinforced responses *increase* the probability that a behavior will be repeated or increased. Behavior that is rewarding to a person will lead to a repetition of a desired behavior.
3. Punishments *decrease* the probability a behavior will be repeated. A behavior that is punished will tend to become extinguished.

MUSIC TEACHERS AND CONDITIONING BEHAVIOR

While both the Watson and Skinner models of behaviorism tried to explain human behavior by conditioning, the music teacher will discover both pros and cons in these approaches regarding performance-anxious students. Certainly, giving rewards and positive feedback to students is desirable when appropriate, but often such feedback is not sufficient to overcome (or condition) the complex mental complexities of chronic, debilitating stage fright.

There are many observable behaviors and nonobservable qualities to consider about all people. At times, negative reinforcement, such as yelling or embarrassing a student, can have an effect of the student trying harder to please, or it can result in the student giving up entirely. At times, little or no reinforcement will create anxiety in students who are looking to others for positive reactions. Some people only feel as worthy as the positive reaction parents, teachers, and/ or the audience show toward them. If reinforcement is not forthcoming, these students will be unable to self-soothe and comfort themselves. Such people have not developed an internal sense of self-esteem, and they crave positive feedback almost exclusively from external sources.

Along with knowledge of reinforcement and conditioning, there are ethical considerations and risks regarding who decides to try to change behavior in another person, why this is attempted, and how this is undertaken. Doing nothing also can be problematic. Change is a complex issue. Students are vulnerable at all ages, and are easily influenced by authority figures, particularly when they are anxious, dependent, and/or needy. Students, like all people, develop their own ways of dealing with anxiety, and they often hold on tight to "old," even if ineffective, ways of resisting change. This can lead to difficulties and impasses both in lessons and recitals. Reinforcement and conditioning techniques as part of teaching technique must be used with an understanding of desired and undesired consequences. Music teachers hold enormous influence with students beyond teaching an instrument. Life lessons are taught in the music studio.

IMPLICATIONS FOR TEACHERS

- Teachers can learn through observation and talking with students which particular triggers are associated with each student's performance anxiety (e.g., seeing audience, waiting backstage, walking on stage.)
- Teachers can assist students in recognizing these stimuli.
- Teachers can pair the anxiety-producing image (stage, audience) with a tension-reducing mental image for performance-anxious students (e.g., performing successfully, image of a favorite pet or person, lying on a warm beach, sitting by a fire, enjoying a vacation).
- Teachers can use knowledge about each student to associate performing with a "custom-made" tension-reducing association. The student can offer special images for use.
- Students should be encouraged to practice mental exercises daily (mentally pairing an anxiety stimulus with an anxiety-reducing association) away from the instrument, studio, and recital hall.
- Teachers will show genuine interest in the student as a unique person.
- Teachers can encourage and reward with compliments both small and large accomplishments of students.

- Teachers will encourage excellence and discourage "perfectionism."
- Teachers will not use sarcasm or harsh critiques when students are having trouble.
- Teachers will help students learn how to find pleasure *within* themselves and not feel good only from external praise and applause.

9

COGNITIVE BEHAVIOR THERAPY,

RATIONAL EMOTIVE THERAPY,

AND LETTER B

QUESTIONS FOR THOUGHT

- What is cognitive behavior therapy (CBT)?
- How does CBT differ from the classical conditioning models?
- How do student statements (Letter B) raise or lower anxiety using a cognitive behavioral model?
- What is the advantage/disadvantage of beta-blocking drugs?
- How can teachers effectively use CBT ideas in the studio?

WHAT IS COGNITIVE BEHAVIOR THERAPY?

Since the 1960s, cognitive behavior therapy (CBT) has become a popular behavioral technique to treat anxiety and other emotional problems. Developed by the psychologists

Aaron Beck (b. 1921) and Albert Ellis (1913–2007), CBT helpfully informs the A B C model of challenging one's anxiety-producing thoughts and behaviors (Letter B) that are believed to increase anxiety. In the case of CBT, emphasis is placed on the patient's irrational thoughts and behaviors at Letter B. The psychodynamic model emphasizes symptoms and ego defenses (Letter B).[1]

Cognitive behavior therapy is focused on what occurs in the present, is time limited, identifies negative thoughts and behaviors (typically called "irrational"), and relabels negative thoughts into positive cognitions. Individuals typically are given homework assignments and are taught specific skills to be employed when anxious and distressed. These skills involve identifying distorted, "irrational" thinking, and self-statements modifying beliefs, relating to others in different ways, and altering behaviors. Cognitive behavior therapy maintains that the self-talk one uses determines how one feels emotionally. For example, a person reading advice in a book (Letter A) might think, "Wow! This sounds good, it's just the information I've always been looking for!" (Letter B) and proceeds to accomplish a task at hand (Letter C). Another

---

[1] Letter B was introduced in previous chapters. It is intended as a model to conceptualize several theoretical ideas besides those involved in CBT. However, the A B C model, presented in previous chapters, typically is associated with CBT approaches and the work of Albert Ellis. I have borrowed the concept of Letter B to conceptualize and illustrate a variety of feelings, reactions, and affects students and teachers experience when dealing with performance anxiety. In this respect, I suggest that Letter B can be explanatory and cross-cut theoretical perspectives.

person reading this same information might think, "Well, this sounds good but I don't think I can do it" (Letter B). The second person may become discouraged and give up (Letter C). The same situation (Letter A), two different people, two different responses (Letter B), and two different results (Letter C) are believed to occur according to one's self-talk (Letter B).

In CBT, underlying motives that fuel self-talk (Letter B) are not explored as they would be in psychodynamic approaches. Rather, according to CBT principles, individual thoughts and statements (Letter B) influence behavior in the present. When people are in distress, their perspective often is considered "irrational" according to CBT theory, therefore thoughts (Letter B) may be negative or unrealistic. Cognitive behavior therapists work with people to identify irrational thoughts that raise anxiety and teach how to challenge and relabel irrational thoughts into positive self statements with the goal of lowering anxiety.

If a student is anxious about memory slips, a CBT therapist would challenge the student's self-statements (Letter B), relabel the self-attributions, and assist the student to develop positive coping statements and behaviors that may reduce this anxiety and alter distorted thinking. For example, if a student insists, "Everyone must like my performance, or I will not be successful" (Letter B), this attitude would be challenged and relabeled into a comment such as, "I hope people enjoy what I have to offer at the piano. However, I cannot guarantee that everyone will like my playing" (Letter B). Changing negative or "irrational" self-statements into positive self-statements maintains that anxiety can be managed better.

The emphasis of CBT technique is directed toward problem solving and changing behavior. Cognitive behavior therapy does not explore the unconscious, or underlying determinants and motivations beneath feelings, symptoms, conflicts, and ego defenses. It is a goal-oriented therapy that includes coaching from the therapist.

AN EXAMPLE OF COGNITIVE RELABELING AND REVISING STAGE FRIGHT RESPONSES

A student may think (Letter B), "My teacher is angry at me because his tone of voice sounded very stern when he corrected my wrong notes." This thought could result in the student feeling anxious and worried. The teacher could help the student identify anxious feelings and relabel them. The student's revised/relabeled response may include (Letter B), "My teacher has no reason to be angry at me, and his comments are not a measure of how he thinks about me. I need to be informed when I play wrong notes. It is important for my teacher to let me know when this happens."

By contrast, a psychodynamic approach would consider that the student had previously felt, or been, rejected by authority figures (parents and/or teachers) and the unconscious reaction by the student might include the feeling that he had done something wrong, felt inferior, and was being reprimanded (ego defenses, Letter B). The student would not be told his thoughts were "irrational,"[2] and he would be encouraged to talk about his anxiety.

Acquiring some basic knowledge about various psychological theories is important for teachers. This information will inform both their attitudes and interventions with anxious students in the teaching studio. For example, from a CBT perspective, a teacher could comment on the student's anxiety and observe the student's negative self-statements while suggesting that the student need not fear criticism from the teacher. From a psychodynamic perspective, the teacher could suggest that the student perhaps had experienced criticism in the past (or, perhaps the student had felt very critical of others), but that the teacher was there to help and not criticize.

Teachers should never try to probe for underlying conflicts. Behavioral approaches are useful in the studio, but it is always helpful for the teacher to realize that there are always many other unconscious issues that fuel performance anxiety before it becomes observable. What is most helpful is the message conveyed to the student that the teacher understands the student's distress, can talk about it, and be a resource for help musically and emotionally.

The activity below was presented in chapter 6, but Letter B responses were dictated by an understanding of ego defenses. The same activity is offered here to illustrate how the A B C model is versatile, and how it can be used for identifying cognitions (Letter B) in the CBT model. This model offers a range of possible concrete options to music teachers and students when dealing with stage fright.

---

[2] According to psychodynamic theories, no thought or feeling is "irrational"; a feeling or thought needs to be explored and better understood in the context of both the present situation and the life history of the person.

TWO ACTIVITIES WITH THE A B C MODEL (EXAMPLE OF CBT)

Activity 1—A B C Recognizing Anxiety Responses

A = performance
B = thoughts, feelings, physical reactions (**cognitions**)
C = consequences (how one performs and self-esteem)

1. Think of a stressful performance (Letter A)

2. What did you say, think, feel about the stressful performance? (Letter B)

Discuss with your teacher or make a list your thoughts, feelings, and body sensations (Letter B).

3. Rate your anxiety (performance "temperature"/Arc of Anxiety)

1 .... 2 .... 3 .... 4 ... 5 .... 6 .... 7 .... 8 .... 9 10
low anxiety   high anxiety

4. Did you use helpful or unhelpful cognitions?

5. List some of the cognitions that you used (Letter B). Discuss them with your teacher.

   1.

   2.

   3.

Activity 2—Rethinking and Relabeling Anxiety Responses

1. Think of a stressful performance (Letter A)

2. What did you say, think, or feel about the stressful performance? (letter B)

3. Rate your anxiety (performance "temperature"/Arc of Anxiety)

0 10
low anxiety   high anxiety

4. Challenge Letter B (i.e., unhelpful cognitions—then respond to Letter B with adaptive cognitions)

5. Rerate your anxiety

1 . . . . 2 . . . . 3 . . . . 4 . . . . 5 . . . . 6 . . . . 7 . . . . 8 . . . . 9 10
low anxiety   high anxiety

6. List some of the adaptive cognitions you used
   1.
   2.
   3.

7. Were the relabeled cognitions effective in lowering your anxiety? Discuss with your teacher.

NEUROPSYCHOLOGY AND BRAIN IMAGING

The study of neuropsychology, brain imaging, and biological psychology, including the effects of drugs on mental functioning, has become a focus for many contemporary clinicians and researchers and holds promise for understanding and treating performance anxiety in the future. Despite the sophistication of imaging the human brain and some important neurological findings that point to anatomical locations of anxiety reactions, these studies typically do not identify what performance anxiety *means* to each individual and/or what emotional and subjective conditions give rise to heightened or lowered emotional arousal. Research done in 2016 by Weinberger and Radulescu suggests that some fMRI[3] findings regarding neuroanatomy and its psychological correlates with emotional functions need to be interpreted with discretion. According to these researchers, because neuroimaging techniques can be highly sensitive to a person's breathing, weight, use of alcohol or drugs, and various other factors, findings are susceptible to being open to doubt or inaccurate altogether. Without a careful understanding of complex confounding issues when interpreting neuroimaging, patients could be inappropriately diagnosed with mental disorders. Future potentials are promising from pursuing collaborative research in these areas.

BETA BLOCKERS AND PERFORMANCE ANXIETY

Drugs called beta blockers reduce or eliminate debilitating physical symptoms of performance anxiety such as

---

[3] fMRI, or functional magnetic resonance imaging, is a type of MRI that measures brain activity through changes in blood flow.

shaking, sweating, and muscle tremors. When an individual is feeling stressed, certain neurotransmitters in the brain release chemicals that cause the heart to beat faster and forcefully. This can have adverse effects on the physical movements required to play a musical instrument. Beta-blocking drugs obstruct these chemicals in the brain so that the heart beats slower and the physical manifestations of anxiety are decreased or eliminated. Propranolol (Inderal) is the beta blocker medication most commonly prescribed for performance anxiety. There are other beta-blocking medications that can be useful for stage fright should Inderal be contraindicated due to one's health history.

Beta-blocking drugs are typically prescribed to treat cardiovascular disease, hypertension, migraine, arrhythmias, and peripheral vascular disease. Because they reduce shaking, sweating, tremor, and other debilitating physical symptoms experienced by anxious musicians, they have been widely adopted by this group. Anxious performers are advised to take this medicine approximately sixty to ninety minutes prior to going on stage. Beta-blocking medications have significantly changed the psychological landscape for many anxious performers. They are considered safe when used correctly and in a proper dose. Beta-blocking drugs are not a miracle cure for performance anxiety, yet they are widely used and, unfortunately, often shared among friends and colleagues instead of obtained from physicians.

All drugs have potential side effects, including very serious ones.

A major benefit of beta-blocking drugs is that, unlike tranquilizers such as benzodiazepines (e.g., Xanax, Klonopin), which cross the blood-brain barrier and can be physically and psychologically addictive, beta blockers do not negatively affect mental functioning. The performer potentially is able to think clearly rather than become drowsy (or drug dependent) as might occur with a mood-altering tranquilizer. The rationale offered for using beta-blocking drugs to manage performance anxiety is that when controlling shaking and other physical impediments to performance, the performer can focus on the music and play in public with decreased emotional duress.

Beta-blocking drugs are not *physiologically* addictive, yet some performers become *psychologically* dependent on them. While physical and psychological dependency have some similar features, physical addition to a drug implies that a particular drug must be used increasingly in higher doses to maintain its desired chemical effect. This kind of drug dependency, or addiction, has potential dangerous physical consequences if certain medications are used in excess and/or abruptly discontinued. Psychological dependency develops a sense of emotional safety and security for some performers when using a drug, such as a beta blocker, and a sense of unease emerges when the drug is discontinued. An important question persists for performers, not often raised, about the use of medication for nonmedical reasons and the underlying meanings of emotional reliance on beta-blocking drugs.

There was optimism that beta-blocking drugs would be an effective "quick fix" for performance anxiety without the negative side effect of affecting mental functioning. This wish has not been borne out. Ironically, because these drugs do not interfere with thinking and cognition, they do not help performers deal with underlying emotional issues of low self-esteem and self-doubt, two of the major debilitating psychological issues that fuel performance nervousness.

One of my patients who tried Inderal for her performance anxiety told me she that began her recital program with the wrong composition. She decided to discontinue using the drug, adding, "I can do that without using drugs." Another felt uninvolved with the music when she used the medication. And although beta-blocking drugs are not supposed to be addictive, particularly in the low dose prescribed for performance anxiety, another of my performance-anxious patients told me that, although she was afraid of using medicine, she licked a beta-blocking pill prior to each performance. She said that it helped her. Some performers consider using drugs for anxiety as a crutch and feel ashamed to try them. Many musicians maintain beta blockers help reduce their performance anxiety and they use them routinely. The research literature on beta-blocking medications typically suggests that if these medications are used that psychotherapy should be combined with drug treatment for the most effective treatment for reducing performance anxiety. This approach emphasizes both mind and body are integral to anxiety reduction.

Since beta blockers are medically used to lower blood pressure, performers who use them for anxiety should be aware if they normally have low blood pressure. A drop in blood pressure that is typically low could induce asthma, dizziness, and heart failure. All drugs, including beta-blocking drugs, must be used with the guidance of a physician who knows one's health history and can fully discuss dosage and treatment options.

EVIDENCE-BASED CLAIMS FOR REDUCING PERFORMANCE ANXIETY

Teachers have access to many psychological resources and numerous lay opinions in the public domain about mental health in today's wellness marketplace. Multiple claims are made by a variety of professionals (and amateurs) for the reduction of stage fright. This information (and misinformation) can be overwhelming and at times, misleading.

The drug and insurance companies are no exception in their participation in our modern healthcare environment. Pharmaceutical and insurance corporations typically cite research supporting "evidence-based treatment" (EBT) as having better outcomes and being more cost-effective than in-depth psychotherapy. While this book is not the place to fully discuss this contentiously debated topic, teachers, parents, and students need to be aware that many cost-effective and "research-based" claims are complex.

According to research on evidence-based treatment, Duncan and Miller (2006), Wachtel, (2010), Shedler (2002, 2010, 2013), Westen (1999), and The American Psychological Association (2013) report that evidence-based findings often are biased and misleading, although at first glance they appear to be attractive, effective, and tidy. It is helpful for music teachers to know about contemporary trends in mental healthcare in order to be informed consumers and trusted mentors for their students.

The final chapter of this book guides teachers through an anxious student's "virtual (mental) recital" and includes both psychodynamic and cognitive-behavioral strategies. This dual focus includes examples of ego defenses and cognitions. Behavior change, insight analysis, and developmental perspectives are offered, when appropriate, by the teacher to the performance anxious student. Teachers, indeed, have important resources in their pedagogical/psychological toolbox when they add psychological instruments to their repertoire.

IMPLICATIONS FOR TEACHERS

- Learn how to use A B C in the CBT model.
- Become aware of student's responses/*cognitions* at Letter B.
- Listen for self-doubts and anxious self-statements at Letter B.
- Help student become aware of what student is saying at Letter B.
- Help student relabel unhelpful Letter B responses.
- Rate anxiety level on a subjective scale of 1–10 (both before and after relabeling level of anxiety).
- Discuss with student the before/after responses and any changes in anxiety levels.
- Repeat this activity many times.
- Compare the range of anxiety responses (low to high) and range of dynamics (soft to loud) to illustrate the variety of feelings and sounds students can experience.
- Encourage students to pay attention to themselves and to become familiar with how they talk and feel about their anxiety (Letter B).
- Help students realize that anxiety can be lowered by how they label their feelings.
- Assist students in developing their own Letter B statements.

10

PERFORMANCE ANXIETY BEGINS

IN THE NURSERY

QUESTIONS FOR THOUGHT

- Where does the student get a first "review"?
- How does knowledge of human psychological development help teachers understand performance anxiety in the studio?
- How can teachers and students use information about psychological development in appropriate and practical ways?
- Limits and boundaries: When is it appropriate for teachers to seek professional help for their students and for themselves?

TEACHERS AS "NEW PARENTS": DEVELOPMENTAL ISSUES

The seeds of stage fright are planted in every person's psychological and physical development at birth. These anxiety seeds can blossom when musicians are faced with a performance stressor at any age.

Development throughout the life cycle, as presented in the important work of the psychoanalyst and educator,

Erik Erikson (1902–1994) is pertinent for music teachers. Erikson's chart "The Eight Ages of Man," has become a classic model for understanding human development through a multidisciplinary biological, psychological, and social lens. In his award-winning book *Childhood and Society* (1950), Erikson maintains that people are capable of psychological growth from birth until the day they die. Erikson's emphasis on lifelong development expands every model of mind and behavior that predates his work and is perennially relevant. Erikson illustrates what he labels "crises" (or conflicts) inherent in each stage of life, how these "crises" develop, and how they can be resolved to promote psychological growth. However, sometimes certain developmental "crises" are not sufficiently resolved, lending to regressive or maladaptive outcomes as one moves inevitably and chronologically through the life cycle. This model also emphasizes how individuals are shaped by their biological, internal, external, and social environments, and how, with proper support, they can move successfully from one stage to another. It is emphasized that every life stage retains both adaptive and maladaptive remnants from previous stages. Life is never perfect. Regressions to earlier stages are likely and even predictable when an individual is under duress—such as public performance.

Erikson's eight stages are cumulative, and each stage is present to some degree at every subsequent stage. A musical analogy is that of Ravel's orchestral masterpiece *Bolero*, where there is a cumulative effect of the music as new instruments are added to the underlying hypnotic rhythm throughout the piece. Or consider the popular song "Twelve Days of Christmas"—each verse includes the previous verse, and all verses accumulate by the twelfth verse. Mental life is like that—themes from first movements and first moments of life are present throughout, as new events, changing relationships, and shifting feelings accumulate throughout the life span. In this respect, mental life is cumulative. Mental life is musical.

Under internal and external pressures, everyone is susceptible to falling backward into old habits (or "crises") from earlier ages. Freud calls this regression. Erikson speaks of lack of resolution of a "crisis." Behaviorists maintain that early experiences are not relevant to their model of the mind. Clearly, the stress of performance anxiety can create the breeding ground for current and distant psychological pressures to emerge for both teachers and students.

Each person composes unique consonant and dissonant mental melodies. It is helpful for teachers to be aware of how the past is represented, often repeated, in the present both by students and by themselves. When considering Erikson's eight stages, the overarching goal for music teachers is to nurture, encourage, and support the development of healthy self-esteem in students. While vital life development in infancy and toddlerhood occurs before students ever meet the music teacher, the music teacher makes important contributions to students' musical and psychological health that build on earlier psychological development, as they become role models and "second" parents.

HUMAN DEVELOPMENT AND PERFORMANCE ANXIETY

When thinking about human development, teaching, and performance anxiety, it is important to understand that young children are not fully developed emotionally or physically. There is a long period of being dependent on caregivers. Children are not "small adults." Their minds are like sponges, and they absorb everything that is said as well as attitudes that are expressed silently by caregivers and teachers. Young children's minds work concretely and often "magically." For example, as her parents were driving her grandparents back to the airport to go home following a visit, a three-year-old child commented, "Gramma and Grampa live at the airport." A young music student may feel, "My teacher didn't smile at me today because she is mad at me." The young child's world revolves concretely around the child's needs, fears, fantasies, beliefs, and wishes; it does not function using logic.

Until a child has a greater command of language, the child expresses feelings through actions and sometimes through emotional outbursts that are labeled tantrums. Tantrums are anxiety-driven behaviors and a display of emotional symp-toms that are communicating a child's message to others. Young children have difficulty distinguishing inner feelings and outer reality. Informed, supportive, and caring adult guidance and nurturance from the nursery throughout the growing years (and beyond) are critical for psychological and musical growth.

The fearful and anxious child will display feelings and actions that may be precursors to performance anxiety in the teaching studio and on stage. Much groundwork is laid in the nursery and childhood before lessons are commenced. It is imperative for both parents and teachers to appreciate that since most students begin piano lessons in childhood, teach-ers are powerful influences on emotional development and psychological safety. Teachers can provide "new parenting" to students of all ages.

Teachers benefit from becoming informed about life-stage milestones that occur long before a young student commences instrument lessons. In this chapter, following a brief description of each of Erikson's eight stages (Figure 10.1), specific points are emphasized that are pertinent to music study, with both adaptive and maladaptive outcomes listed, depending on the child's temperament and upbringing. The

STAGE	AGE (years)	CRISIS	FAVORABLE OUTCOME	TASKS
1	Birth-1	Trust vs. Mistrust	Hope	Feeding, Nurturing
2	2-3	Autonomy vs. Shame and Doubt	Will	Potty Training, Walking, Talking
3	4-6	Initiative vs. Guilt	Purpose	Exploration
4	7-12	Industry vs. Inferiority	Competence	School, Skill Development
5	13-19	Identity vs. Role Confusion	Sense of self	Social Relationships
6	20-34	Intimacy vs. Isolation	Love	Love Relationships
7	35-65	Generativity vs. Stagnation	Creative Work, Parenthood	Accomplishments, Nurturance
8	65...	Ego Integrity vs. Despair	Wisdom	Reflection, Fulfillment

FIGURE 10.1 Eight Stages of Development
(Adapted from Erik H. Erikson's "Eight Ages of Man" Epigenetic Chart in *Childhood and Society*)

impact of development on performance anxiety is emphasized in the context of human development over the course of the lifecycle.

One's earliest days and years create a lifelong foundation for the emergence of performance anxiety at any age. Self-esteem and healthy self-regard is the antidote for shame, humiliation, fear of abandonment, and many issues around competition that are blatantly prevalent in the formation of the dynamics of stage fright. Each student is a unique individual with a biological endowment and a personal life history long before and after he or she plays the first note on his or her instrument. The importance of sensitive guidance and attitudes that music teachers provide students cannot be overemphasized.

ELABORATION OF ERIKSON'S EIGHT STAGES OF THE LIFE CYCLE

<u>Relationships</u> <u>Favorable/Unfavorable Outcomes</u> <u>Basic Life Tasks</u>

Stage 1—Trust vs. Mistrust (birth–one year)
Infant/Mother   Hope/Insecure   Feeding/Nurturing

Stage 2—Autonomy vs. Shame and Doubt (two-three years old)
Toddler/Parents   Potty/Walk/Talk Doubts   Self-control

Stage 3—Initiative vs. Guilt (four–six years old)
Preschool/Family   Exploration/Inhibition   Purpose/Initiative

Stage 4—Industry vs. Inferiority (seven–twelve years old)
School age/Teachers/Friends Skill/Doubt   Competence/Confidence

Stage 5—Identity vs. Role Confusion (thirteen-nineteen years old)
Adolescence/Peers   Sense of self/Confusion   Secure Sense of Self

Stage 6—Intimacy vs. Isolation (twenty–mid-thirties)
Young Adult   Companionship/   Work/Relationships
                     Love/Exclusion

Stage 7—Generativity vs. Isolation (mid-thirties–mid-sixties)
Mid-adult   Accomplishments/   Creative Pursuits/
                     Impoverishment   Parenting

Stage 8—Integrity vs. Despair (sixty-five ....)
Late Adult   Wisdom/Despair   Reflection/Fulfillment

Stage One—Trust vs. Mistrust (Birth-One Year Old)

The newborn takes in the world. This first experience in life primarily occurs through the infant's body. The infant's mouth, eyes, ears, and skin literally "take in" the world through vision, hearing, eating, and body sensations. Parents supply these psychological nutrients through their care, reliability, and attention to the baby's needs. The newborn is totally dependent on others for his or her existence. Responses by others to the infant's cries and sounds shape lifelong attitudes toward the self and others, along with a feeling that the world is primarily a reliable place where needs are met. If overly indulged or neglected, the infant could become mistrustful of those around him and of his own abilities to influence others later in life.

Infant/parent "paradise" is lost for the first time (in a healthy way) when the baby is appropriately weaned and learns that every cry does not elicit an immediate response. The baby has to wait for gratification and develop tolerance for delay, frustration, and self-soothing. How this situation is handled in infancy can lead to feelings of emotional "starvation" or emotional self-soothing and self-satisfaction. A need for love and nourishment, literally and psychologically, from others provides the groundwork for all subsequent emotional growth. One gradually finds the capacity to love oneself, which is a healthy resolution of Trust vs. Mistrust.

In positive situations, there is a mutual regulation between parent and child. This creates a healthy balance between trust and mistrust in the child's internal and external world. People care. They are reliable. They do not leave you. If people leave, they return. The child develops a capacity to feel secure.

IMPLICATIONS FOR TEACHERS

- Teachers need to realize that they automatically become both positive and negative mental representations of parents, since students experience teachers as "parent figures."
- Teachers should promote an atmosphere of tolerance and persistence in students to assist careful learning. Learning music takes time, patience, working through mistakes, and steady support, particularly when students become frustrated.
- Teachers need to instill hope that students can overcome learning difficulties as well as musical and emotional setbacks.
- Teachers need to be aware of the relevance of feeling rejected and understand students' worry about not being good enough (or perfect) when performing as a fear of being rejected.

- Teachers should be aware that applause is a metaphor for receiving earliest parental love and nourishment.
- Teachers should help students appreciate that in reality things can turn out "OK" even when everyone, including the performer, is not "perfect."

Stage Two—Autonomy vs. Shame and Doubt (Two-Three Years Old)

The baby becomes a toddler with all the rights and privileges of the two-year-old. To stand up vertically and no longer crawl horizontally on the floor, and to stand on one's feet to walk, is to experience the world from an entirely new perspective both physically and psychologically. In Stage Two, the toddler walks and talks and can begin to let go of some of the necessary dependency inherent in infancy. These are the years labeled the "terrible twos," when the child realizes that the child is separate from the parents and not just an extension of them (of course the toddler cannot articulate this but demonstrates feelings through actions and self-assertion.)

The toddler conveys his individuality by saying "No," implying "I am different and separate from you" (the parent). The acquisition of speech and words lends power to the toddler's mobile explorations of the world and of himself. Potty training involves both letting go of something from inside one's body and, simultaneously, gaining control over one's body in doing so. To accomplish this healthy developmental task can bring a great sense of accomplishment and pride for the toddler—or it could lead to power struggles with the parent, and, over time, with others. Such developmental struggles can lead to conflicts within the mind and in relationships.

Both Stage One and Stage Two set the earliest stage for adaptive (or maladaptive) attitudes toward performing, teachers, and audiences. The conviction of being loved (despite playing "wrong notes") and being accepted as a separate valued human being contribute mightily to confidence in performing on stage. Early derivatives of performance anxiety, including loss of control of memory and technique, often can be traced back to the first few years of life and how these issues were navigated in the child–parent relationship. A healthy sense of oneself and developing age-appropriate autonomy are positive results of the tasks the toddler faces.

The outcome of Stage Two can result in a sense of autonomy but also lead to shame and doubt should there be unresolved difficulties. Feeling comfortable with separations, with one's body, and self-assertion/autonomy accompany a performer on stage. Positive outcomes of earliest relationships allow the student to experience the audience and the teacher as the "good" parent. An undesirable outcome of toddlerhood is to be susceptible to feelings of shame and doubt, since the child may fear a parent, teacher, or audience responding, "Shame on you"!

IMPLICATIONS FOR TEACHERS

- Teachers need to understand how dynamics of Stage Two affect the student's growing sense of self as more independent and to assist those students who lack confidence.

- Teachers should encourage students to explore and experiment at their instrument and to develop opinions about music.
- Teachers need to appreciate student complaints about "boo boos," "dropped notes," and "messy technique"— verbal expressions about mistakes and remnants of toddler potty training and potty talk—and help students realize that mistakes are not "bad," "disgusting," or "dirty." Mistakes are learning opportunities.
- Teachers should discourage self-limiting behaviors and "can't do" attitudes.
- Teachers should help the student feel proud as a whole person.
- Teachers should listen for (and point out, when necessary) student comments that indicate the student is ashamed of himself in the lesson or complain that a performance is not "perfect."

Stage Three—Initiative vs. Guilt (Four–Six Years Old) and Stage Four—Industry vs. Inferiority (Seven–Twelve Years Old)

These years involve the psychosocial tasks of playing games with others, obtaining pleasure in learning, and the development of conscience about right and wrong versus being self-absorbed and critical. There is pleasure gained in learning new ideas, going to school, curiosity about where babies come from, and beginning to notice the difference in size and gender of other children and adults. Parents and teachers become role models for emerging attitudes and behaviors.

Many children begin private lessons during one of these two life stages. The inclination for competition also evolves—with peers and parents—which extends eventually to other musicians when performing. Less positive outcomes find the child feeling purposeless and inferior, displaying general anxiety and low self-esteem, and possibly feeling guilty about being unsuccessful or even guilty when feeling successful. With good-enough (notice the word "perfect" is not used) guidance from teachers and parents, preadolescents (and parents) can move through this period with greater self-awareness and self-confidence. The successful negotiation of Stages Three and Four bodes well for performing before others and enjoying the experience. Teachers are in a unique position to identify anxiety in students from early ages at lessons.

ANXIETY ALERTS FOR TEACHERS!!!!!
Young Students:
- May cry or become clingy.
- May not want to come to lessons or have their parent leave them alone with the teacher.
- May have tantrums or become quiet and withdrawn.
- May develop stomachaches or other physical pains before lessons/performances.
- May tell the teacher she/he is scared—(or may show anxiety through avoidant behaviors instead of words.)

Middle School Age Students:
- May become self-conscious.
- May worry things will turn out badly.
- May not be able communicate directly to teachers using words.
- May miss lessons (that often compete with soccer, basketball, volleyball, or other social and sport activities).

- May want to quit lessons altogether and/or not play in recitals.

IMPLICATIONS FOR TEACHERS

- Teachers can take advantage of the beginning student's energy and motivation to learn new things.
- Teachers need to be aware of the self-judgments students often place on themselves—particularly a harsh, demanding, and critical superego about being "bad" or "wrong."
- Teachers should be aware that they are important role models.
- Teachers can promote healthy attitudes toward competition and use disappointments as teachable moments.
- Teachers need to realize the power of peers and promote collaboration, for example, through chamber music and duet playing.
- Teachers can help preadolescents appreciate the physical and emotional changes that are occurring in their bodies and minds as integral to developing pride and self-confidence at their instrument.
- Teachers can help students not to be overly concerned with "what others think."
- Teachers can foster a healthy sense of identity— "who am I?"—in students.

Stage Five—Identity vs. Identity Confusion (Thirteen-Nineteen Years Old)

In Stage Five, the teenager has to cope with important issues which include the questions "Who am I?" and "What do I think?," acceptance by peers, and entrance into meaningful relationships, often romantic ones. It is during this stage that adolescents become more or less serious about music, and by the end of the teen years, some have decided on careers in music, which helps solidify a budding sense of identity. These years potentially result in immense growth socially, psychologically, physically, and musically. Music students who, by this time, have been playing an instrument and working with a private teacher for years, and who feel accepted by peers, potentially have developed a deep ego investment in learning and performing music. For adolescents who have major struggles with emerging sexual and developing occupational interests, conflicts at this stage between childhood and adulthood can be quite stormy. As will be evident to the observant teacher, earlier life experiences have accumulated significantly by this period. Self-esteem, personal identity, and performing are tightly linked with personality development and relationships with others.

ANXIETY ALERTS FOR TEACHERS!!!!!
Adolescents:
- Students may focus increasingly on themselves and be preoccupied with what people think of them.
- Students may have difficulty interacting with other teenagers and/or adults.
- Students may become intensely involved in peer groups.
- Students may worry about who will be in the audience.
- Students may want to be thought of as "cool" yet come across as "indifferent."
- Students may make choices about advanced university or conservatory training.

- Students may have conflicting views about career choice with those of parents.
- Students may be ambivalent about their choice to pursue music.

IMPLICATIONS FOR TEACHERS

- Teachers should organize studio activities where students can feel a part of a group experience.
- Teachers must be aware of peer pressure and the attraction of activities other than music, including a social life, that may divert music students from practicing or from taking lessons altogether.
- Teachers should be aware of adolescents' concerns about their body- and self-image and how this affects performing in public.
- Teachers should be aware of the adolescent's age-appropriate struggles with questions like "Who am I?" and "What do I feel?"—which may include commitment (and/or ambivalence) to further or professional music study at college.

Stage Six—Intimacy vs. Isolation (Twenty–Mid-Thirties)

Psychological development is described throughout the life cycle to illustrate age-appropriate tasks that are pertinent in the teaching studio at all stages of life. It is evident that the vicissitudes of later life are built on early and ongoing development.

During the years of young adulthood, ranging between ages twenty and thirty, the intensity of youthful friendships evolve into intimate romantic relationships replete with the vulnerabilities that come from revealing oneself to another person (for the performer, revealing oneself to the audience). Mutual love and admiration is a marker of such relationships. It is during this stage of life that musicians have a deep relationship with music and make a serious commitment to it as a "life partner." Work choices become increasingly important and related to one's sense of self and self-esteem. Performance anxiety results when there are impediments or triggers—psychological, physical, and/or social—that interfere with these needs. If there is a regression or emotional backsliding, it has been influenced by earlier stages in life, where development was thwarted due to unresolved problematic life events or emotional circumstances.

If previous development, including relationships with parents, peers, and teachers, has gone well enough, most performers are able to deal with the challenges of the intensity of performance demands, including the ability to deal with anxiety without becoming overwhelmed. For those individuals who have not mastered the conflicts and crises of earlier stages in development, there is increased potential that the demands of young adulthood will be considerable, and the musician may retreat from performing.

Fears about loss of the self (symbolized for performers as loss of technique or memory) can result in avoidance behavior and feelings of loneliness and isolation. The performer may worry that the audience will not love him. Therefore, a serious commitment to performing may be highly conflicted or circumvented altogether. A career that includes music performance offers many built-in external challenges

that tap into developmental dynamics of rejection and competition. However, performing gives immense satisfaction.
Those who pursue it find challenges to one's vulnerability
worth the effort, and performing ultimately can be gratify-
ing. At times, performing enables individuals to successfully
cope with complex past personal history.

IMPLICATIONS FOR TEACHERS

- Teachers of this age group are likely working with
  serious musicians intent on a career at a university
  or conservatory program.
- Teachers need to have an appreciation for the musician's deep involvement and identification with
  music as well as the impact of occupation on one's
  sense of self.
- Teachers need to appreciate that many early issues
  around love, acceptance, rejection, and competition are
  revived in important ways for an individual intent on
  pursuing music professionally in a career where jobs are
  scarce, often not well paying, and highly competitive.
- Teachers need to appreciate that sometimes there is
  a struggle within the musician about remaining in a
  music career after many years of focused work.

Stage Seven—Generativity vs. Stagnation
(Thirty-five–Sixty-five Years Old)

The mature musician continues to contribute to the next
generation through teaching and creative activity, which
includes performing. The musician may decide to write

articles or books so that his/her ideas can be disseminated in publications. In building a legacy for future generations, transmitting knowledge and sharing music through teaching, concertizing, and writing are important links from one's past to future generations of musicians.

It is not unusual for instrumentalists who have begun lessons in childhood, but discontinued playing for many years, to restart studying their original instrument. Some people decide to learn new instruments or to collaborate with colleagues by playing more chamber music. Musicians may still be active in their profession, but they also may begin to think of redirecting or expanding their musical activities as they anticipate life changes in the years ahead. It is not unusual for creative endeavors to reach a peak at this stage.

Regression to a problematic stance at this stage would result from feeling impoverished for a lack (or perceived lack) of creative success in earlier years. This may result in becoming self-absorbed or even depressed. Interestingly, some musicians have spent so many years being creative and productive that they have lost the capacity to enjoy a meaningful personal life outside their studios. In spite of their professional productivity, these musicians may feel despondent or lonely.

IMPLICATIONS FOR TEACHERS

- Teachers should be aware of the motivations and interests of older adult students who pursue (or restart) an instrument at later stages in life.
- Teachers need to be aware of their own stage in the life cycle, and their motivations for nurturing

students who may be returning to music study after years of working in another occupation.

- Teachers should feel proud of their contribution to society through music teaching and fostering creativity in students.
- Teachers should be aware of the importance of the musical and pedagogical legacy they will leave to future generations.

Stage Eight—Integrity vs. Despair (Sixty-five–)

There is serious reflection on one's life at this age. Balancing fulfillment versus bitterness and satisfaction versus regrets are emotional tasks that confront every person who lives into older adulthood. Often there is a pursuit of new and creative activities, and decisions are made about retiring—or not retiring. The momentous choices made at this stage include considerations about how life has been lived, and thoughts about planning for the future. These highly personal evaluations impact feelings about encroaching old age and eventual non-being. It is also a time of reflection and looking back on one's life, which includes both satisfactions and disappointments.

An openness to all kinds of creative expression and additional gratifications awaits the teacher and performer who has reached this stage of artistic and chronological maturity. Yet navigating the unknowns of retirement and beyond present unique challenges for musicians who have spent many years working with others, often in institutions of higher education or managing a private studio. Years of familiar routines of daily life become new avenues for opportunity, different for each person. The teacher has a chance to consolidate past challenges of work and personal experiences that have ripened over a lifetime. For those musicians who have navigated the challenges of careers with a sense of satisfaction, there is a feeling of pride. For those who feel they have fallen short of their goals and who feel more regret than pleasure, there is despair and remorse because life will not last long enough to start over. There is great poignancy in the knowledge that each teacher has spent a life in music.

Retirement proverbially is always in the future until one day, it becomes "now." Interestingly, one may retire from an occupation, but one never retires from (or tires of) being a musician. The psychological and occupational paths that intertwine for teachers and performers are never more poignant than at the beginning and end of one's career. Retirement is a time of interesting potential for new activities and also the time for the realization of life's limitations. Retirement, like graduation, is both an ending and a beginning—a beginning and an ending.

IMPLICATIONS FOR TEACHERS

- Teachers can reflect on their own sense of professional and personal fulfillment in music.
- Teachers can reflect on their careers as they look ahead toward retirement.
- Teachers can find new creative outlets and activities.
- Teachers can enjoy hearing former students perform and enjoy success.
- Teachers can know they made a difference in many lives.
- Teachers can appreciate their own life in music and take pride in a job well done.

RECAP: DEVELOPMENTAL STAGES AND STAGE FRIGHT

Teachers can glean considerable wisdom about their students and about themselves from Erik Erikson's contribution regarding lifelong development. In his model, "The Eight Ages of Man," there is emphasis on the cumulative effects of the first years of life, biological endowment, family dynamics, and society over the course of an entire lifetime. Multiple influences shape our personhood. Among the major influences for music students is the music teacher, a metaphorical parental substitute.

Since most students begin lessons during elementary school (or sometimes at younger ages) and perform in recitals at very young ages, feelings about oneself are set into motion by a combination of family, social, and biological factors. The attitudes acquired from early years arrive with the child in the teacher's studio at the first lesson and accompany the child on stage during the first (and all subsequent) recitals. How the child has been nurtured (or not), been allowed to healthily separate from parents (or not), been allowed to have independent ideas (or not), been allowed to become an individual in his own right (or not), and been valued by others and valued himself (or not) sets the trajectory for varying levels of performance anxiety. Experiences in significant relationships, social influences, and biological endowments affect the student's capacity to cope with love, rejection, shame, competition, and guilt. These markers of psychological personal identity accompany the young, preadolescent, teenaged, young-adult, middle-aged, and elderly person at every music lesson and in each public performance from birth to death.

As noted by Erikson, favorable outcomes at all stages of life lead to resilient and confident individuals who are better equipped emotionally to withstand the rigors of anxiety and myriad external and internal pressures. Both nature *and* nurture are emphasized. As such, Erikson's theory about development is useful for teachers, parents, coaches, and many others. It is important to keep in mind that none of the eight stages has an entirely positive or negative outcome (Erikson called the outcome of each stage a "ratio" or balance). A favorable progression through each stage (and help from others when struggling) results in the mental strength to cope successfully with life crises. An unfavorable outcome would likely result in mistrust, self-doubt, depression, and anxiety, including debilitating performance anxiety.

Music teachers significantly can help fill and repair gaps for some of the inevitable difficulties faced by their students during their formative and mature years. No one has a "perfect" childhood. Teachers can assist anxious and self-doubting students. The music teacher's goal is to provide a safe atmosphere for learning, to promote self-esteem, to encourage confident performers, and to share the pleasures of making music. As such, teachers can have profoundly influential (and often life-altering) relationships with all of their students.

ADDITIONAL IMPLICATIONS FOR TEACHERS

Teachers need to consider the following ideas about performance anxiety regardless of student age or theoretical foundation:

- Performance anxiety can be mystifying and painful for performers of all ages.

- An understanding of the connection between psychological development and music development is important.
- Shame and embarrassment are emotional and social components of performance anxiety.
- Reassurance and reasoning does not eliminate students' dread of experiencing an emotional and technical meltdown in public.
- Students often are reluctant to talk about anxiety. Teachers can provide a safe and supportive place for this topic to be explored.
- Performance anxiety frequently is considered a "stigma" or personal "flaw."
- Performance anxiety typically is *not* a musical problem.
- Increased hours of practice (especially if students sit mindlessly at their instrument while mechanically going over the same music) will not "fix" stage fright.
- Avoidance and less practice will not solve anything.
- Teachers can help students lower performance anxiety significantly when adding psychological skills to their musical repertoire.

11

A "VIRTUAL" RECITAL

A Synthesis

QUESTIONS FOR THOUGHT

- How can teachers coach students to help them psychologically prepare for recitals?
- How can teachers use information about psychodynamic and behavioral theory in their pedagogical "toolbox?"
- What is a "virtual recital?"
- What are the benefits of a "virtual recital?"

SUSAN: HOW TO *UNDERSTAND* AND *HANDLE* PERFORMANCE ANXIETY

In this chapter, a teacher coaches an anxious student through a "virtual" recital using an imaginary dialogue about stage fright based on a synthesis of the information presented in previous chapters. The strategies employed involve *behavioral* (cognitive behavior therapy, or CBT) and *psychodynamic* approaches to typical student responses (Letter B).

The imaginary student, Susan, has practiced hard for her recital. She has talked about her fears about shaking, sweating, cold hands, "what people will think of her," fears of memory slips, and technical meltdowns. Her teacher has been a good listener and allowed Susan to feel safe talking about this "dangerous" topic.

Susan's stage fright affects her self-esteem and undermines her excellent musical preparation. Sometimes she worries about being "crazy," because her anxiety feelings are so strong, and they frighten her. Her friends and some relatives have told her, "If you are smart, intelligent, and practice hard you should be able to perform well. Don't worry about it." After all, isn't it supposed to be true that "smart people can solve their own problems?"

Susan does need to practice hard but also needs to practice wisely and with focus. There is no absolute *guarantee* that accidents will be avoided even when preparation is exemplary. Susan's teacher can help her lower her anxiety by adding some psychological techniques to her music technique.

CONCEPTS FOR THE TEACHER TO CONVEY TO SUSAN, THE RECITALIST

- Emphasize that anxiety is a *normal* feeling, and that Susan definitely is *not* crazy.
- Encourage Susan to express her feelings verbally about the recital.
- Offer some ideas about how to make anxiety work *for her.*
- Listen to Susan's thoughts but do *not* suggest they are off limits or that being anxious makes her less of a person or musician.

- Offer Susan some mental strategies to help her deal with her musical strategies that have already been worked on in her lessons.
- Help Susan learn to *control her performance anxiety.* Performance anxiety does not have to bully her!

PLAN FOR THE TEACHER

- Go through a "virtual" recital (a mental recital away from the instrument) with Susan. Susan will not play a note, but will use her imagination. Susan will vividly and verbally imagine that she is preparing, and then she will imagine herself performing on stage.
- The teacher will challenge Susan's initial responses when they are self-deprecating (Letter B) and *re*evaluate them (Letter B) with Susan to help her devise alternative, helpful ways of dealing with her anxiety. Susan will probably discover rather quickly that she is her own harshest critic—even though, at first, she may be focused more on what others think about her (*hint:* worrying about what others think raises one's anxiety and is probably connected to what one thinks about oneself. No one can forecast what others are thinking. None of us is a mind-reader!)

FORMAT OF "VIRTUAL RECITAL"

A performance is designed for Susan. Susan and her teacher can plan this together. A typical "anxious response" for each section of the recital is supplied by Susan; this includes feelings and thoughts that raise her anxiety level (Letter B). Next the teacher offers Susan *two* alternative replies to Letter B that can help lower Susan's anxiety (i.e., relabel Letter B).

Teachers will realize quickly that how one *thinks* about oneself (Letter B) and how one *feels* about oneself (Letter B) will have a powerful impact on the level of performance anxiety (refer to the Arc of Anxiety Model and the ABC Model). It is not mind over matter. Attitude and aptitude, music and mind working together really matter!

How to **handle** performance anxiety provides a cognitive-behavioral (CBT) perspective about performance anxiety at Letter B. Teachers help students challenge negative, unhelpful self-talk. How to **understand** performance anxiety presents a psychodynamic perspective on performance anxiety at Letter B. Teachers help students challenge nonadaptive ego defenses. Both approaches first empathize with Susan's anxiety-raising responses at Letter B and subsequently offer relabeled anxiety-lowering responses at Letter B.

Letter A represents the recital. The consequences of anxiety-raising or anxiety-lowering self-talk are represented by Letter C, namely, the quality of performance and the pleasure/fear the student experiences. The responses offered in Susan's virtual recital are typical and illustrative of performers' self-dialogue at Letter B. These self-statements offer the teacher a way to conceptualize and use psychological theories with students as alternative responses to anxiety. It is recommended that the teacher not repeat the responses given here verbatim, but rather use them to develop psychological understanding that will frame each teacher's responses to specific student needs.

Integrate ideas that are meaningful for you and your students. Custom-create some personal situations, responses, and ideas in collaboration with your students. Add different scenes. Have students propose items and responses. The "virtual recital" can be presented to students in groups or individually. Over time, students can coach each other. Present one or two scenarios at a time so students can discuss and digest them thoroughly before moving on to the next performance situation. Start at the beginning and do not jump around, since scenarios are designed to become progressively more anxiety arousing.

When the teacher understands underlying issues, perspectives on how to intervene will be enhanced. The teacher should not try to be a therapist but should be aware that there is more occurring in the student's mind than a focus on the right notes. At times, it helps to talk about some rudimentary psychological concepts with students. Teachers should always feel welcome to consult a mental health professional to help with teaching psychological issues. Student confidentiality is always a primary concern. As always, it is important for teachers to keep appropriate boundaries regarding the student's emotional life and to refer to a professional should the teacher believe that a serious or chronic problem exists.

In the "virtual recital," each question is to be vividly mentally imagined by Susan, and her replies are then addressed by her teacher. Two sample teacher responses follow every response that Susan offers. To reiterate, how to *handle* anxiety offers a cognitive-behavioral (CBT) perspective on Susan's replies. How to *understand* anxiety offers a psychodynamic perspective on Susan's replies. Both perspectives illustrate Letter B responses, but they are derived from two different theoretical perspectives. The teacher and student are encouraged to create a recital situation that is unique to their circumstances.

The audience is seated, the lights are dimmed, Susan imagines she is backstage . . .

Let's begin.

THE RECITAL

Question: What would you say if . . .

YOU WERE SCHEDULED TO GIVE AN IMPORTANT RECITAL IN THREE WEEKS?

Student: I am worried that I will not be adequately prepared and will not make a good impression, and people won't like me. My friends will make fun of me. I need more time to practice.

Teacher response: How to *Handle* Anxiety (CBT)

Teacher: There are three weeks left to get ready. Use your time wisely and practice mindfully. You have worked hard already. Now is time to fine-tune. Think positively about yourself and focus on the music instead of thinking about your friends. You cannot control what other people think, but good friends will not make fun of you.

Teacher response: How to *Understand* Anxiety (Psychodynamic)

Teacher: Your anxiety may reflect old fears about how the audience and your friends (who in some respects represent your parents in a displaced way) can love or leave you based solely on how you perform. You want to please your family—that is natural. How you perform in a recital does not determine the love people have for you.

Question: What would you say if . . .

TWO WEEKS BEFORE YOUR PERFORMANCE, YOUR FRIENDS OFFER SUGGESTIONS ABOUT YOUR REPERTOIRE AND QUESTION YOUR TEACHER'S ADVICE.

Student: They must know something I don't know!! Maybe my teacher forgot to tell me something important, and my friends know something I don't know. What should I do now?

Teacher response: How to *Handle* Anxiety (CBT)

Teacher: At this point, do not change your approach. Evaluate other suggestions after your performance. There are many ways to prepare and play music. This is *not* the time to have self-doubts and negative thoughts. It *is* the time to trust your preparation and ability.

Teacher response: How to *Understand* Anxiety (Psychodynamic)

Teacher: While validation from others is important, this is the time to believe in your strengths, feel good about yourself, and know that you have prepared as well as you can. It is time to think about what is *right* with you instead of worry about what is *wrong with you*. It is OK if friends have different ideas—you *are* different and separate people.

Question: What would you say if . . .

ONE WEEK BEFORE THE PERFORMANCE YOU TRY OUT YOUR PROGRAM FOR A SMALL AUDIENCE. YOUR TECHNIQUE FAILS YOU IN A SPOT THAT HAS NEVER CAUSED TROUBLE BEFORE.

Student: Oh no!!! Suppose this happens the night of the performance! I feel panicky. I'd look so stupid. Feel embarrassed. Humiliated. I must calm down. I'm going to ask my doctor to give me a prescription for a beta blocker. That drug will help me relax.

Teacher response: How to *Handle* Anxiety: (CBT)

Teacher: You are trying too hard. That mistake never happened before. Analyze musically what happened. Try some muscle relaxation and deep breathing. Focus on what you need to do—don't give in to anxiety. Take a deep breath slowly . . . now exhale. Keep it slow and steady. Try it several more times. Notice how slow, deep breathing makes you feel calmer and peaceful. More relaxed.

Teacher response: How to *Understand* Anxiety (Psychodynamic)

Teacher: A beta-blocking medication will probably help your shaking and physical anxiety symptoms, but it will not stop your self-doubts in your mind. You wish for a magic pill, but there is no magic pill. It is important to understand how your body is speaking through your physical symptoms.

Question: What would you say if . . .

IT IS THE EVENING OF YOUR PERFORMANCE. YOU ARE WAITING BACKSTAGE. THE FIVE-MINUTE WARNING BELL SOUNDS. . . .

Student: This pressure is horrible!! I've got to suck up my feelings and perform well. Why is this happening to ME? Why does performing seem so much easier for other people?

Teacher response: How to *Handle* Anxiety (CBT)

Teacher: Think about sharing what you know you can do. Try some relaxation. Breathe deeply. Visualize a relaxing scene: a beach, a vacation, a special event, cuddling a pet. Visualize a successful performance. You have practiced doing this kind of mental exercise every day. Use these mental techniques now. You will *share*, not *prove*, your love of music. Communicate something to your audience. Feeling anxiety is normal. It is what you say about anxiety that makes a difference.

Teacher response: How to *Understand* Anxiety (Psychodynamic)

Teacher: It is not helpful to compare yourself with other people and how they perform. Everyone is different. That is good. It would be helpful to understand your competitive motivations. People can feel jealous of others. Feeling competitive is OK. Competition can be motivating. Think about yourself as successful. Give yourself permission to succeed (and make mistakes) without believing you are awful and a failure.

Question: What would you say to yourself if . . .

YOU ARE WALKING ON STAGE. YOUR RECEIVE A WARM OVATION FROM THE AUDIENCE. . . .

Student: I must perform well enough to justify this ovation. The audience expects me to perform well.

Teacher response: How to *Handle* Anxiety (CBT)

Teacher: You control anxiety better when you have faith in yourself and concentrate on what you are doing instead of your self-doubts. Trust your preparation without negative thoughts about what can go wrong. Your brain is a reliable computer that remembers what you put into it. Enjoy this performance. Even when you play your personal best, there is no guarantee that everybody will like your performance. The audience is greeting you and welcoming you with applause.

Teacher response: How to *Understand* Anxiety (Psychodynamic)

Teacher: The audience represents many people who have been important in your life, specifically your parents and teachers. You do not want to disappoint any of them. It helps to realize that the audience represents the "critic" inside your own head. It will help for you to be your own best fan instead of your own worst critic.

Question: What would you say to yourself if . . .

AS YOU BEGIN YOUR PERFORMANCE, YOUR ARMS FEEL WEAK AND SHAKY AND YOU NOTICE YOUR HAND ARE COLD.

Student: I'll never be able to get through this program with cold, trembling hands. I would be so much better off without these physical symptoms. My body is betraying me.

Teacher response: How to *Handle* Anxiety (CBT)

Teacher: Let's get rational! These physical symptoms are giving you a cue to cope—use positive self-statements. Take a deep breath, concentrate, and play the best you can. Focus on the music. Use your mind to help your musical technique. This is the time to trust in your good practice habits.

Teacher response: How to *Understand* Anxiety (Psychodynamic)

Teacher: Your body is reacting to what is going on in your mind, and your mind is responding to what you feel in your body. Your body and mind are closely connected. You are focusing now on the physical aspects of anxiety. Perhaps this represents you feeling ashamed, exposed, transparent, and judged as inadequate by others. Performers often have dreams of being laughed at for not being good enough and looking funny. Your body is revealing what your mind is trying to conceal. These are powerful emotions. They do not have to undermine you when you can recognize them.

Question: What would you say to yourself if . . .

JUST WHEN YOU FEEL LESS NERVOUS AND YOUR PERFORMANCE IS SUCCESSFULLY UNDERWAY . . . YOUR MIND FLASHES TO A TRICKY SPOT COMING UP SOON.

Student: Just when I am calming down and things are going well **this** happens. I am worried about that tricky passage.

Teacher response: How to *Handle* Anxiety (CBT)

Teacher: You have tried this program for friends and it went well. You played it in studio class. You have prepared the difficult passages with great care and concentration. Focus on what you are playing right here and now. Breathe deeply. Stop overthinking. Let it flow.

Teacher response: How to *Understand* Anxiety (Psychodynamic)

Teacher: If you are too good technically or musically, you may have a fantasy that you will be "punished" for your wish to be superior. So you have a mistake and sabotage your success. Performance accidents are the way to punish yourself and not allow yourself be as good as you can be. Then you feel guilty, and this feeling undermines performing. Is your fear of failure camouflaging your underlying fear of success? Are you afraid others will be jealous if you play well? You can use an understanding of your feelings to work for you not against you. It can feel wonderful to be successful—enjoy your performance.

Question: What would you say to yourself if . . .

YOU ARE NEARING THE END OF YOUR PERFORMANCE. YOU ARE PLAYING WELL. SUDDENLY, YOU HAVE A MEMORY SLIP.

Student: #@)&*^^_>*!!&!'""!!!!!!

Teacher response: How to *Handle* Anxiety (CBT)

Teacher: Use your mind!!! Don't panic! Flash to a relaxing scene—a beach, a fuzzy animal, a person who is comforting. This accident does not make you a terrible person or performer. You can handle this and move on. Keep going— you have prepared for this kind of thing. You have a "jam plan." Use it. There is no such thing as a perfect performance.

Teacher response: How to *Understand* Anxiety (Psychodynamic)

Teacher: You made a "boo boo," you had an "accident." These statements are things a young child might say about an embarrassing potty accident—listen to the words you are using to express being afraid of mental and physical loss of control with a memory slip. You are not a toddler—but those embarrassing toddler-feelings can emerge anytime at any age for anybody who experiences stress about performing. How humiliating and shameful that feels. You are no longer that toddler—you can use your in-depth knowledge about yourself to cope with those feelings now.

Question: What would you say to yourself if . . .

YOU RECOVER FROM THE MEMORY SLIP AND END THE PERFORMANCE ADMIRABLY

Student: I am surprised I played as well as I did. The audience seems so appreciative.

Teacher response: How to *Handle* Anxiety (CBT)

Teacher: There were good reasons to expect the performance would go well. You were prepared. You had rehearsed mental and musical strategies every day and played your program in trial performances many times. You used focused relaxation and mental imagery and you used anxiety as a cue to use coping strategies. These tools helped. You can feel good that you added mental skills to your musical skills. They will come in handy in many life situations besides playing the piano.

Teacher response: How to *Understand* Anxiety (Psychodynamic)

Teacher: Sometimes feeling good about your performances is difficult because you feel independent when on stage. Feeling independent, which you enjoy, can also raise worries about separation from your parents. To feel competent may activate the idea that your parents will no longer need you (or you won't need them!)—at least in the same way you needed each other when you were a helpless baby and vulnerable little child. This is normal healthy growth. Performing is helping you grow. Success on stage can enhance your self-esteem. Enjoy your accomplishments.

IMPLICATIONS FOR TEACHER AND RECITALIST

All of the psychological information in the "virtual recital" is theoretically and clinically sound. It is helpful to empathize with students about what they are experiencing as well as to offer additional ideas (previously discussed in the studio and studio classes) of which they are not aware in the moment. When coping perspectives offer alternatives to panic and anxiety responses (Letter B), typical feedback includes:

- "It helps to realize how I drag myself down with anxiety."
- "It helps so much to put my thoughts and feelings into words."
- "When I realized I didn't have to be *perfect*, my anxiety diminished and I enjoyed performing."
- "It is useful to understand where my anxiety comes from in my mind."
- "It helps so much when I can talk about what I feel rather than keep it inside my head" (comment of ten-year-old girl).

Teachers can help students lower anxiety when students (and any of us) sense that they are listened to, are encouraged to express feelings in a safe environment, and feel understood.

12

RECAPITULATION AND FINALE

QUESTIONS FOR THOUGHT

- How will you use cognitive behavior therapy (CBT) **and** psychodynamic ideas in your teaching?
- Can you identify ways you can help students with their performance anxiety without being a professional psychologist?
- Has your understanding of performance anxiety changed or deepened?
- Can you design some custom-made strategies for helping your performance anxious students?

PUTTING IT ALL TOGETHER

The process of guiding Susan through her imaginary performance with **How to *Handle* Anxiety** strategies employed a combination of systematic desensitization, visualization, relabeling negative self-statements, and focused breathing, which are cognitive behavior therapy (CBT) techniques. **How to *Understand* Anxiety** emphasized recognizing symptoms and ego defenses, emotional conflict, and other principles regarding unconscious determinants as explained by psychodynamic theory. Mental techniques can help students lower anxiety, but teachers need to emphasize that students need to practice coping strategies and examine their attitudes regularly, just as students practice their instrument regularly. Teachers then can offer strategies and ideas that are appropriate to the age and interests of students and coach students to discover helpful alternatives to unhelpful Letter B statements. Teachers should use judgment and tact when offering a "virtual recital." The overarching goal is to enhance self-esteem and promote resilience at all ages and levels of playing.

For example, if a young child is hesitant to leave mother or tells the teacher he is scared, the teacher can

- Talk with the child about the instrument as a new friend, perhaps asking the student to give his friend a "name."
- Convey the message that being scared (or whatever words the student uses) is not unusual and explore with the student what is so scary.
- Use dolls, stuffed animals, or puppets to act out a pretend performance.
- Suggest that a teddy bear or favorite doll sit on the piano bench with the student.
- Play a duet with the student.

A middle school-aged child may worry about mistakes and start to miss lessons as a recital approaches. The teacher can

- Express curiosity about the student's absences in a nonjudgmental way.
- Try to understand if and how the student is worried about lessons or performing.
- Invite another student (or the teacher) to play a duet with the student.
- Encourage the student use music at the recital.

A teenage student may feel anxiety about what others will think and worry about who will be in the audience. The teacher can

- Explore worries with the student.
- Offer some alternative ways of thinking about performing.
- Suggest that the student does not have to prove any-thing but is sharing the music.
- Find examples online of famous nervous performers to share with the student and help normalize the feel-ing of anxiety.
- Allow the student to use music in the performance.

A university music major has made a big commitment to a career path. Sometimes, there is uncertainty about this choice. Certainly coming to a music school as a young adult requires many adjustments besides music study with a new teacher. One important adjustment involves being away from home, interacting with peers who may or may not be more comfortable performing, needing to manage time indepen-dently and effectively, and being exposed to new ideas—musical, social, and academic. It is a time of huge personal growth and separation from the family of origin. Students will be aware of what others think and are eager (sometimes conflicted) to establish a musical and personal identity. The teacher can

- Realize she is a role model and life coach in many ways at the university, where programs dedicated to music student wellness, and particularly the psychol-ogy of performance, sadly are lacking.

- Help the student explore music and life goals, including rethinking some long-held beliefs.
- Help students balance emotional and psychological independence and the requirements necessary for skills to develop as a musician.
- Be careful not to become so invested in having competition "winners" in order to bolster teacher's reputation, but prepare students to compete confidently as part of the healthy development of the student.
- Realize that all previous life experiences are part of the mental and musical repertoire that are present psychologically in university music school students.

Teachers will quickly realize that shaky self-esteem at any age, both off and on stage, is accompanied by negative thoughts such as "What will other people think about me?," "I will feel ashamed," "Will I make a fool of myself?" Physical symptoms such as shaking, sweating, tense muscles, and catastrophic beliefs and ego defenses such as "I can't do this" or "Maybe I should stop playing my instrument" will also become evident. It is helpful for teachers to recognize how students experience lessons as a performance and teachers as quasi-parents. Teachers must remember that they too were once students, and that they continue to learn from their students and colleagues. Teachers and students of all ages need to realize that performance anxiety is a self-worth issue and not only a musical problem.

It is not unusual for symptoms and conflicts to become manifest as physical and psychological expressions of thoughts and emotions that have been harbored unconsciously for many years. By the time students experience symptoms of performance anxiety, the original stimulus has become displaced or repressed (forgotten) from an original event, relationship, memory, or feeling. Performing on stage is a powerful trigger that emotionally ignites difficult buried feelings specifically around issues involving being loved, wanted, approved, competing, and winning/losing—all basic to psychological human development and self-esteem on and off stage.

Vignette: Steven

One talented teenager, Steven, harbored the fantasy since early childhood that he was responsible for his parents' divorce because he cried when they left him with a babysitter. Steven recalled that his parents did not go out with each other very often. He believed his outbursts caused his parents to argue and finally to separate. He found solace in playing his violin. Over time, he became afraid to assert himself on stage or in other situations where people could stay or leave, like and audience or his parents. Steven's early symptom of crying evolved gradually (and unconsciously) into associating crying and making mournful sounds on his instrument. This belief seeped into his stage fright reactions by adolescence. Steven gradually was helped to understand that he had nothing to do with his parents' problems, and that the sounds he made with his instrument would not cause people to leave him or ridicule him. Steven's sense of omnipotence about having the power to break up his family became redirected into pleasure in his competence when playing his violin. With the help of a therapist and a sympathetic and informed music teacher, his anxiety became significantly lower.

PERFORMANCE ANXIETY IS MORE THAN SYMPTOMS

The energy of the mind that surges beneath its surface can play mental "tricks," and students can develop symptoms far removed from any actual instigating event. Although Steven's music teacher was tuned-in psychologically, this student needed more in-depth psychological work to not feel guilty, and to develop a capacity to enjoy performing on stage and feeling happy off stage. Steven's performance anxiety brewed long before it reached his teacher's studio, the stage, or the psychologist's office. Unacknowledged and untreated, anxiety can interfere seriously with pleasure in performing and prevent students from reaching both music and life goals. The importance of the music teacher's role in making appropriate referrals cannot be underestimated or overemphasized.

Musicians are diligent at working hard and practicing for long hours. A "work/practice harder" ethic does not necessarily produce emotional comfort in performance. In such cases, it is important to recognize that relentless, chronic, debilitating symptoms of performance anxiety are serving as a "disguise" for some unresolved issues that *propel* the "problem" that is subsequently labeled performance anxiety and stage fright.

Unlike an approach that uses cognitive techniques to relabel negative self-statements (which can also be considered ego defenses), a psychodynamic approach to performance anxiety assesses performance anxiety to be more than a symptom that can be removed, with new labels replacing old thoughts. In the "virtual recital," *understanding* Susan's performance anxiety was rooted in psychodynamic principles. That is, the possible multiple origins of the fears that accompanied her on stage were available in the informed teacher's mental tool kit to better understand how to listen and work with her. The music teacher did not do psychotherapy, however, with her empathetic comments.

Listening carefully and trying to understand students are powerful anxiety reduction tools. When the teacher listened to Susan's responses about her performance, she was focusing on Susan's "Letter B" answers both in *handling* (offering suggestions for relabeling self-talk) and *understanding* (hearing beneath the surface of symptoms).

STIGMAS, CAUTION, AND OPTIMISM

A stigma about mental illness prevails in our society, although fortunately less so than in years past. The diagnosis of a physical problem is still more "acceptable" than a diagnosis of anxiety or depression. People would not hesitate to seek treatment for a heart attack, but they do not rush to psychotherapy for a broken heart. Many people who engage in psychological treatment for performance anxiety benefit from working through long-held convictions that being in psychotherapy means they are "crazy," "stupid," or "dumb," or that they just don't work hard enough. As a result, these people of all ages can find emotional anchors inside themselves that are helpful in times of stress, such as appearing in public. In fact, these pessimistic beliefs about oneself typically are embedded in self-esteem issues that can surface as stage fright.

Some words of caution and optimism are offered regarding both cognitive and psychodynamic theory and treatment.

It is important to realize that brief, cognitive therapy can be misused just as lengthy, in-depth therapy can be misused. One can focus on short-term "solutions" to avoid long-term determinants. Conversely, one can dwell on past issues to avoid making changes in the present. The notion of a "perfect" anxiety-free performance (or perfect teacher or perfect therapist or perfect family) is a fantasy, not a reality. Teachers can help students appreciate and accept their assets *and* their limitations.

TUNING IN TO STUDENTS AND TUNE-UPS FOR TEACHERS

Teachers must become aware of symptoms they detect in students and also cognizant of attitudes within themselves. While the student is at the center of the teacher's pedagogical attention at all stages and ages, the teacher needs to become aware of any personal actions or attitudes of his own that may prevent psychological attunement in the teacher–student dyad. The following questions need to be addressed seriously and periodically by all teachers.

- Are some teachers favoring some students and not others?
- Are some teachers reacting harshly with their comments and demands to students?
- Are some teachers too involved in building and sustaining their own reputation and assign inappropriate repertoire for a student's level, particularly concerto repertoire for competitions?

- Are some teachers competing with other faculty for students and professional prestige—using their students to bolster their reputation?
- Are teachers supportive or competitive colleagues?
- Do some teachers entice talented students from a colleague's studio into their own?

The music teacher is often the "first responder" to music students. Yet, teachers must be "first responders" to their own mental health before they can be effective in the studio and classroom.

INTERDISCIPLINARY COLLABORATION

A great deal, particularly regarding attitudes toward performance, career, mental health, relationships, and lifestyle (including nutrition and exercise), can be emphasized sensitively in the studio, studio classes, and classrooms. However, as noted, there are times when teachers must refer students to mental health or medical professionals. Music teachers, mental health, and medical professionals need to collaborate in *interdisciplinary collaboration* about complex problems that are presented in teaching studios and consulting rooms.

- It is important that teachers not feel it is a "weakness" (in the student or in themselves) or believe that they have "failed" in some way or will be exposed as incompetent if a referral is made.

- It is a strength to seek appropriate professional help, and for teachers to recognize that they cannot be all things to all students.
- Mental health awareness should be included in teacher training programs and at faculty in-service meetings and seminars.
- Teachers and mental health professionals (who have expertise in treating performers) should have access to each other for formal and informal consultations.
- Teachers should invite mental health professionals into their studio classes and classrooms on an ongoing basis to dialogue with students.
- Teachers should not try to be "armchair" psychotherapists to their students. Therapists should not try to be "armchair" teachers to their patients. This is dangerous psychologically and crosses ethical boundaries.
- It is *imperative* that referrals and the work done in therapy be kept strictly *confidential*. Students should never feel that this information will be shared or made public in any way—to the teacher, administrators, or others except in a situation where the student would be considered to be a threat to self or others. In this event, established protocol would be followed.

CRITERIA FOR MAKING A REFERRAL FOR PROFESSIONAL HELP

Teachers cannot be all things to all students. Teachers should refer students, of any age, to a mental health professional for an evaluation when teachers become aware that there is a *chronicity* in the following issues for students:

- Repeated physical complaints with no physical diagnosis.
- Avoidance of practicing, missing lessons repeatedly, backing out of recitals and juries, repeated illness or injury at time of performance or jury.
- Difficulties regulating emotions and behavior connected with sleeping, eating, studying, playing, socializing, and/or emotional equilibrium.
- Performance anxiety that is not modified by rational advice, proper practice, and tryout performances in studio classes or other trial venues. (Complex and deeper mental health issues involving anxiety and depression frequently are masked beneath the symptoms of performance anxiety.)
- Student has serious ongoing issues with rejection and competition (external realities in the competitive music profession which often are residues of internal and interpersonal issues from early childhood).
- Any and all references to harming oneself (including lightheartedly joking about hurting oneself or injuring another person).

MUSIC SCHOOL CURRICULUM

For those students who are training for a professional career in music performance at a university or conservatory, administrators and teachers must offer formal courses and programs in the psychology of performing. Such programs would be

- Well-designed, interdisciplinary, and sensitively implemented wellness programs.
- Taught by experienced and qualified professionals both in and outside the music profession.
- Required in the curriculum (not electives) for all performance majors.
- Available to all music students, in addition to performance majors, for whom these classes are required.
- Equal in importance to courses on music history, music theory, and other required courses in the curriculum.
- Eligible to receive academic credit.
- Funded to cover salaries and teaching materials.

With a lifelong commitment to a career in the performing arts coupled with the difficult job market following extensive and expensive higher education, those who teach musicians and administer education programs are failing their students if they do not prepare students *emotionally* as well as musically and technically for career opportunities and challenges that follow graduation.

Every student must be recognized as a whole human being who is greater than the sum of his or her (musical) parts. Each student takes a unique life history into the private studio, into classes, on stage, and outside the walls of the music school. The teaching studio, classroom, and concert hall can reactivate early, but buried, painful emotional conflicts that come alive during the young adult's formative years spent in higher education. Psychological intervention, when appropriate, must be encouraged as an option and promoted as a strength. Psychologically informed teaching and/or effective treatment can make a difference in both the short- and long-term health of the student.

It is the ongoing challenge and opportunity of those who educate musical performers to provide resources and funding for student mental health at school **and** through referrals to appropriate mental health professionals. In the current economic and social climate, audiences for classical music, in particular, are diminishing, and income for many musicians has stagnated or deteriorated. This makes musicians an "at risk" population. Can music schools afford not to take sensible, sensitive, bold, and creative steps to educate their graduates to be emotionally healthy performers and cultural ambassadors of the future?

CODA: SUMMARY OF GUIDELINES FOR RECOGNIZING AND TEACHING PERFORMANCE ANXIETY REDUCTION

- Normalize performance anxiety—make the private lesson a safe place for you and your student to talk about stage fright as part of music-making.
- Listen to what students say—do not try to convince them they should not be nervous. It may be helpful to share information about famous performers, public speakers, or actors who have spoken about their performance nerves, such as pianist Vladimir Horowitz, violinist Isaac Stern, opera singer Renee Fleming, or some popular performers such as Barbra Streisand,

Beyonce, and Adele. There are numerous articles on Google about musicians, actors, athletes (and others), and stage fright.

- Help students become aware of what students think, feel, and say to themselves about performing. Point out self-defeating, conflicted, and negative self-statements.
- Talk about performance anxiety with students individually *and* in studio classes.
- Teach how to use anxiety effectively as a cue to cope (use examples about school, home, friends) with Letter B responses.
- Practice A B C strategies in studio classes when students play for each other. Help students recognize ego defenses, cognitions, feelings, and conflicts (Letter B).
- Realize that several psychological theories can be informative for student responses at Letter B.
- Invite students to be "performance coaches" for each other.
- Let students know that it is "cool" to talk about what they feel in a safe environment. (What is said in class stays in class!)
- Invite students to offer constructive suggestions or share experiences with their classmates in a *nonjudgmental* manner. (It takes time to develop a studio group-safety atmosphere.)
- Invite students to offer suggestions about what makes the studio class a safe place to speak.
- Emphasize that "perfection" is a myth—there is no such thing as "perfection" except in our wishes and imagination. There is no "perfect performance."

- Emphasize that there are competent performers, not omnipotent performers.
- Customize what works best for each student at each age level.
- Involve and teach parents about child development, anxiety cues, and learning tools.
- Organize a parents' class a couple of times a year. Invite a mental health professional to join or lead the class and to be available year-round as a resource.
- Develop working relationships with mental health professionals in the community for teacher consultation or referrals when necessary.
- Respect boundaries and privacy.
- Refer to a mental health professional when teaching tools are not helpful. Do not try to become a therapist-teacher.

At times, all of us need help from others. If students can trust and rely on others, they can learn to trust others and rely on themselves when on stage. Trust is an important lesson for teachers to share with music students as it pertains to life lessons. Adaptive attitudes involving life lessons will greatly enhance performance anxiety management.

UNIQUENESS OF MUSIC TEACHERS' ROLE

Teachers can be most effective psychologically with their students when doing what they do so well—LISTEN. Listen to students' mental music (what they say about how they feel and think) as well as their instrument playing. Music teachers have a uniquely special role in students' musical and psychological lifelong development. While teachers cannot be parents and should not be psychologists for their students, they can be effective listeners, coaches, and role models.

There are a variety of psychological tools to handle and understand performance anxiety. While it would be ideal if the needs of each person could be matched to a personal formula, it would be an overstatement to claim that every coping technique and every theory works for everyone in every circumstance. In mental and musical life there are no "formulas." The mind is always active and reactive. Performance, too, is a living and breathing art. There are always unknowns when a student, or anyone, performs on stage. The unknown also can create excitement about performing in public.

Teachers have a unique opportunity to teach *and* illustrate by their personal example of self-care, healthy self-esteem, and self-love as an integral part of studying and performing music. The variety of approaches to handling performance anxiety gives teachers options for creating a versatile mental/musical toolbox. The more students use and practice the options available to them to build their own mental repertoire, the more secure students will feel when performing musical repertoire.

Do not be misled by the thinness of this book and equate brevity with simplicity. Volumes could be written about any of the concepts discussed. Performance anxiety is serious and can affect both personal and professional dreams and ambitions. Stage fright can create havoc with self-esteem, motivation, and performance for music students and for teachers. Handled and understood with compassion and with knowledge, stage fright can be used to enhance performance.

▼

13

DA CAPO

Back to the Beginning

I DID NOT KNOW ANYTHING about psychotherapy or psychoanalysis when I experienced stage fright at Juilliard many years ago. It was not a topic that was discussed. Stage fright was endured.[1] Like all music students, I learned about concepts such as consonance, dissonance, ambiguity, conflict, resolution (musicians analyze these elements as harmonic and formal structures in the score), and multiple function (musicians call this counterpoint and harmonic modulation). Years later, however, music analysis enabled me to resonate with psychoanalysis, which also uses the terms consonance, dissonance, ambiguity, resolution, and multiple function. I learned how to analyze a score from multiple perspectives, to listen carefully, and to become aware of musical interpretations. I practiced the piano for long hours. I performed in many recitals. I did not learn about managing my performance anxiety.

I did not enter psychoanalysis overtly because of my stage fright, yet my performance anxiety became an important topic of exploration for me. I realized how my stage fright had affected many areas of my life. Through my curiosity about

---

[1] Juilliard now has a career center and counseling service that assists students with psychological issues and job concerns.

myself and others, my music teaching, my clinical work and research, and my personal psychoanalysis, I came to understand my first memory slip and its significance regarding my shame about my "forever recording." I now understand how my little white toy piano, the beloved gift from both my parents when they were married, held lifelong powerful meaning for me. I needed to mourn some of the contrapuntal melodies in my mind. One of these mournful melodies was the realization that I could not recover the traumatic "forever loss" of my father's sudden abandonment shortly before I started piano lessons. A brilliant performance could not undo what occurred. Nor would a stellar performance cause my father to return.

My fantasies and shame around forgetting became transformed into anxiety about loss, feeling forgotten, and not feeling good enough when I attempted to express myself at the piano on stage. I had to face the music of the disillusionment of my omnipotence and unrequited yearnings for an intact family and find pleasure in what I *could* have and *could* accomplish. I have come to appreciate that, for me, combining my music and psychoanalytic training have been deeply satisfying and have permitted me to bring together and share with others two disciplines that, at first glance, appear unrelated—like my parents after their divorce.

Teachers can significantly help their students since they, too, are in the mental health profession by virtue of their caring occupation working in a one-to-one relationship (or classroom) with students over extended periods of time. Because of this unique, close, and lengthy relationship, it is always important to remember that boundaries and level of psychological training be respected in working with the inevitable emotional aspects of performance. By adding informed and sensitive psychological understanding to a music pedagogy toolbox, teachers not only will help their students become more confident performers and resilient recitalists but also will discover greater pleasure in teaching.

GLOSSARY OF PSYCHOLOGICAL

TERMS USED IN THE TEXT

Every professional discipline has its own language and labels to provide shorthand recognition for frequently used but highly complex phenomena. For example, music teachers are familiar with using single words to convey complicated concepts and instructions to their students such as "allegro," "lento," "crescendo," "pianissimo," "accelerando," "ritard," and "sforzando". All of these words provide a specialized shortcut vocabulary that suggest more detailed and nuanced ways to think about intricate musical issues. Shortcut words also are employed by psychologists to connote specific yet multilayered ideas about behavior, thoughts, and emotions.

The major psychological terms that are used in this text, while not comprehensive in the psychological lexicon, are defined in this glossary. They are useful as a tool for teachers to keep in mind when working with students to try to better understand students and themselves.

These psychological concepts inherently are neither good nor bad. They are not diagnostic. They are descriptive. All of these psychological terms may be used adaptively and maladaptively, consciously and unconsciously by individuals. Many concepts typically are used simultaneously. When the teacher or student observes such behaviors, it is not appropriate or helpful to be judgmental but rather to observe what is said and help the student (and oneself) realize how consideration of formal concepts may be useful toward self-understanding. It is not the presence or absence of a particular quality, but the degree to which thinking, feeling, and behaving might assist or undermine an individual and affect performance.

Specific examples of every concept in this glossary have been provided throughout this book. Concise and shortened definitions of psychodynamic terms are offered here, extracted from the excellent volume *Psychoanalytic Terms and Concepts* edited by Burness Moore and Bernard Fine (1990). Page numbers are listed for detailed reading if desired by readers. Behavioral concepts have been culled from Diana Kenny's book *The Psychology of Music Performance Anxiety* (2011). No attempt is made to critique or compare theories, terms, and concepts in the Glossary.

Classical Conditioning: "(Pavlov, 1927) describes a learning situation in which neutral objects are paired with noxious events, called unconditioned stimuli, in such a way that the neutral objects take on the properties of the noxious unconditioned stimuli, thereby producing the same reaction that would normally be elicited by the noxious stimuli alone." (Kenny, 2011, p. 116)

Cognitive Behavior Therapy (CBT): "underpinned by the proposition that emotions and behavior are influenced by cognitions (i.e., beliefs or ideas about oneself and others). In CBT, therapists evaluate, challenge, and assist patients modify false or distorted cognitions associated with their symptomatic behavior." (Kenny, 2011, p. 179)

Cognitive Relabeling (Restructuring): "concerned with changing faulty thinking patterns that give rise to maladaptive behaviors, such as excessive muscle tension, avoidance of feared situations, or impaired performance, adaptation, and coping. In this therapy, people learn a skill called cognitive restructuring, which is a process whereby negative, unproductive, or catastrophic thinking is replaced with more rational, useful ways of understanding problem situations." (Kenny, 2011, p. 182)

Conflict: "*Psychic* or *intrapsychic conflict* refers to struggle among incompatible forces or structures within the mind, *external conflict* is that between the individual and aspects of the outside world. (They often go together)." (Moore & Fine, 1990, p. 44)

Conscious: "A quality of mental awareness (consciousness) of external events and mental phenomena." (Moore & Fine, 1990, p. 45)

Countertransference: "A situation in which an analyst's feelings and attitudes toward a patient are derived from earlier situations in the analyst's life that have been displaced onto the patient. Countertransference therefore reflects the analyst's own unconscious reaction to the patient, though some aspects may be conscious." (Moore & Fine, 1990, p. 47)

Denial: "A primitive or early defense mechanism by which an individual unconsciously repudiates some or all of the meanings of an event (sometimes called *disavowal*). The ego thus avoids awareness of some painful aspect of reality and so diminishes anxiety or other unpleasurable affects." (Moore & Fine, 1990, p. 50)

Displacement: "Shifts the focus or emphasis in dreams and behavior, generally by diverting the interest or intensity attached to one idea onto another idea that is associatively related but more acceptable to the ego." (Moore & Fine, 1990, p. 48)

Ego Defense: "a general term describing the ego's active struggle to protect against dangers . . . during development and throughout life." (Moore & Fine, 1990, p. 48)

Isolation of Affect: "Separates a painful idea or event from feelings associated with it, thereby altering its emotional impact." (Moore & Fine, 1990, p. 49)

Multiple Function (Multiple Determinism): "A construct stating that a psychic event or aspect of behavior may be caused by more than one factor an may serve more than one purpose." (Moore & Fine, 1990, p. 123)

Operant Conditioning: "In operant conditioning (Skinner, 1953), the person must make a response, i.e., operate on his environment, in some way. If the response is followed by a reward, called positive reinforcement, then that response is more likely to occur again in a similar situation. However, if the response is punished, the occurrence of the response becomes less likely in future." (Kenny, 2011, p. 118)

Projection: "Externalizes the objectionable impulse or idea by attributing it to another person or to some perhaps mystical force in the outside world." (Moore & Fine, 1990, p. 49)

Psychoanalysis: "A branch of science developed by Sigmund Freud and his followers, devoted to the study of human psychology. It is usually considered to have three areas of application: (1) a method of investigating the mind; (2) a systematized body of knowledge about human behavior (*psychodynamic theory*); and (3) a modality of therapy for emotional illness (*psychoanalytic treatment*)." (Moore & Fine, 1990, p. 152)

Rationalization: "A process by which an individual employs subjectively 'reasonable' conscious explanations to justify certain actions or attitudes while unconsciously concealing other unacceptable motivations." (Moore & Fine, 1990, p. 160)

Reaction Formation: "Changes the unacceptable to acceptable, thereby also ensuring the efficient maintenance of repression. A painful idea or feeling is replaced in conscious awareness by its opposite." (Moore & Fine, 1990, pp. 48–49)

Regression: "A return to a more developmentally immature level of mental functioning." (Moore & Fine, 1990, p. 164)

Repression: "A defensive process by which an idea is excluded from consciousness." (Moore & Fine, 1990, p. 166)

Resistance: "A paradoxical phenomenon regularly encountered in the course of insight-oriented psychotherapy, particularly psychoanalysis. The patient, who has sought professional help to uncover neurotic problems, opposes the process in a variety of ways that would serve to defeat the objective of change. . . . Resistance may take the form of attitudes, verbalizations, and actions that prevent awareness of a perception, idea, memory, feeling, or a complex of such elements that might establish a connection with earlier experiences or contribute insight into the nature of unconscious conflicts." (Moore & Fine, 1990, p. 168)

Symptom: "Psychoneurotic symptoms are caused by unconscious psychic conflict arising from contending forces within the individual. . . . Such unconscious conflict is universal and unavoidable, and childhood instinctual conflicts do not always cause symptoms." (Moore & Fine, 1990, p. 193)

Transference: "The displacement of patterns of feelings, thoughts, and behavior, originally experienced in relation to significant figures during childhood, onto a person involved in a current interpersonal relationship. Since the process involved is largely unconscious, the patient does not perceive the various sources of transference attitudes, fantasies, and feelings (such as love, hate, and anger). Parents are usually the original figure from whom such emotional patterns are displaced, but siblings, grandparents, teachers, physicians, and childhood heroes are also frequent sources." (Moore & Fine, 1990, p. 196)

Unconscious: "Mental content not available to conscious awareness at a given time, as demonstrated by parapraxes, dreams, and disconnected thoughts and conclusions. The mind is always active, performing many functions during both the waking state and sleep, but only a small amount of this mental activity is conscious at any one time." (Moore & Fine, 1990, p. 201)

ILLUSTRATIVE READINGS

ON PERFORMANCE ANXIETY

American Psychological Association. (2013). Recognition of psychotherapy effectiveness. *Psychotherapy, 50,* 102–109.

Beck, A. T. (1975). *Cognitive therapy and emotional disorders.* Madison, CT: International Universities Press, Inc.

Bourgeois, M. D., & James A. (1991). The management of performance anxiety with beta-adrenergic blocking agents. *Jefferson Journal of Psychiatry, 9*(2), Article 5. Retrieved from http://jdc.jefferson.edu/jeffjpsychiatry/vol9/iss2/5

Duncan, B. L., & Miller, S. D. (2006). Treatment manuals do not improve outcomes. In J. C. Norcross, L. E. Beutler, & R. F. Levant (Eds.), *Evidence-based practices in mental health: Debate and dialogue on the fundamental questions* (pp. 140–149). Washington, DC: American Psychological Association.

Ellis A. E., & Harper R. A. (1975). *A new guide to rational living.* Englewood Cliffs, NJ: Prentice-Hall.

Erikson, E. H. (1950, 1963). *Childhood and society.* Second edition. New York, NY: W. W. Norton.

Fishbein, M., & Middlestadt, S. E. (1987). The ICSOM medical questionnaire. *Senza Sordino, 25,* 1–8.

Freud, S. (1915–1916). *Introductory lectures on psycho-analysis.* Standard Edition, Vol. 15 (James Strachey, Trans. and Ed., 1963). London, UK: Hogarth Press.

Freundlich, D. (1968). Narcissism and exhibitionism in the performance of classical music. *Psychiatric Quarterly, 42*(Suppl), 1–13.

Gabbard, G. O. (1990). *Psychodynamic psychiatry in clinical practice.* Washington, DC. American Psychiatric Press.

Gabbard, G. O. (1997). The vicissitudes of shame in stage fright. In C. W. Socarides & S. Kramer (Eds.), *Work and its inhibitions: Psychoanalytic essays* (pp. 209–220). Madison, CT: International Universities Press.

Horvath, J. (2015, October 20). A musician afraid of sound. *The Atlantic* (Health).

Kelly, V. C., & Saveanu, R. V. (2005, June). Performance anxiety—How to ease stage fright. Current Psychiatry, 4(6). Retrieved from http://www.currentpsychiatry.com/home/article/performance-anxiety-how-to-ease-stage-fright/40ca615e9165e7348a 2870639197051c.html

Kenny, D. T. (2011). *The psychology of music performance anxiety.* Oxford, UK: Oxford University Press.

Lansky, M. R., & Morrison, A. P. (Eds.). (1997a). *The widening scope of shame.* Hillsdale, NJ: Analytic Press.

Lansky, M. R., & Morrison, A. P. (1997b). The legacy of Freud's writings on shame. In M. R. Lansky & A. P. Morrison (Eds.), *The widening scope of shame* (pp. 3–40). Hillsdale, NJ: Analytic Press.

Lewis, H. B. (1971). *Shame and guilt in neurosis.* New York, NY: International Universities Press.

Lockwood, A. (1989). Medical problems of musicians. *New England Journal of Medicine, 320,* 221–227.

Meichenbaum, D. (1978). *Cognitive behaviour modification.* New York, NY: Plenum Press.

Moore, B., & Fine, B. (1990). *Psychoanalytic terms and concepts.* New York, NY: American Psychoanalytic Association, Vail-Ballou Press.

Morrison, A. P., & Stolorow, R. D. (1997). Shame, narcissism, and intersubjectivity. In M. R. Lansky & A. P. Morrison (Eds.), *The widening scope of shame* (pp. 63–87). Hillsdale, NJ: Analytic Press.

Nagel, J. J. (1988). In pursuit of perfection: Career choice and performance anxiety in musicians. *Medical Problems of Performing Artists, 3*, 140–145.

Nagel, J. J. (1989a). Musicians' maladies (Correspondence). *New England Journal of Medicine, 321*, 51.

Nagel, J. J., Himle, D. P., & Papsdorf, J. (1989b). Cognitive-behavioral treatment of musical performance anxiety. *Psychology of Music, 17*(1), 12–21.

Nagel, J. J. (1990). Performance anxiety and the performing musician: A fear of failure or a fear of success. *Medical Problems of Performing Artists, 5*(1), 37–40.

Nagel, J. J. (1991). When good teaching isn't enough. *American Music Teacher, 40*(4), 16–17, 71.

Nagel, J. J. (1993). Stage fright in musicians: A psychodynamic perspective. *Bulletin of the Menninger Clinic, 57*, 492–503.

Nagel, J. J. (1996). Stressbusters for music teachers. *Piano and Keyboard, 183*, 19–23.

Nagel, J. J. (1998a). Injury and pain in performing musicians: A psychodynamic perspective. *Bulletin of the Menninger Clinic, 62*(1), 83–95.

Nagel, J. J. (1998b). Injury and pain in performing musicians: A psychodynamic diagnosis. In R. T. Sataloff, A. G. Brandfonbrener, & R. J. Lederman (Eds.), *Performing arts medicine* (2nd ed., pp. 291–299). San Diego, CA: Singular.

Nagel, J. J. (1999). When is a music teacher more than a music teacher? Psychological issues in the studio (invited article). *American Music Teacher, 48*(6), 10–13.

Nagel, J. J. (2004). Stage fright theory and treatment: One size does not fit all. *Medical Problems of Performing Artists, 19*(1), 39–43.

Nagel, J. J. (2006). Performance anxiety and the musician. *The American Psychoanalyst (TAP), 40*(2), 16, 22.

Nagel, J. J. (2007a). Freud meets Mozart on the oral-aural road. *The American Psychoanalyst (TAP), 41*(4), 22, 33.

Nagel, J. J. (2007b, Winter). Convert performance anxiety into performance energy. *Keyboard Companion*, 38–39.

Nagel, J. J. (2007c). Melodies of the mind: Mozart in 1778. *American Imago, 64*(1), 23–36.

Nagel, J. J. (2008a). Psychoanalytic perspectives on music: An intersection on the oral and aural road. *Psychoanalytic Quarterly, 77,* 507–530.

Nagel, J. J. (2008b). Psychoanalytic and musical perspectives on shame in Donizetti's *Lucia di Lammermoor. Journal of the American Psychoanalytic Association, 56,* 551–563.

Nagel, J. J. (2008c). Book Review: *Violin Dreams* by Arnold Steinhardt. *Journal of the American Psychoanalytic Association, 56,* 1371–1376.

Nagel, J. J. (2008d, January 27). Survival of music and arts is critical to our nation's well-being. *Ann Arbor News,* A-16.

Nagel, J. J. (2008e, February). Culture, community, and change. *Farmington Gazette,* p. 16.

Nagel, J. J. (2009). How to destroy creativity in music students: The need for emotional and psychological support services in music schools. *Medical Problems of Performing Artists, 24*(1), 15–17.

Nagel, J. J. (2010). Psychoanalytic and musical ambiguity: The tritone in "Gee, Officer Krupke." *Journal of the American Psychoanalytic Association, 58,* 9–25.

Nagel, J. J. (2013). *Melodies of the mind.* London, UK: Routledge.

Nagel, J. J. (2015–). Mind matters. *Clavier Companion.* Monthly column.

Nagel, J. J. (2015, March/April). Harmonizing the psychological and physical pain in performing musicians. *American Music Teacher,* 31–33.

Nagel, J. J., & Nagel, L. (2005). Animals, music, and psychoanalysis. In S. Akhtar & V. Volkan (Eds.), *Cultural zoo: Animals in the human mind and its sublimations* (pp. 177–206). Madison, CT: International Universities Press.

National Endowment for the Arts. (2014). *The National Endowment for the Arts announces new research on arts employment.* Retrieved from http://arts.gov/news/2014/national-endowment-arts-announces-new-research-arts-employment#sthash.nMTHmgL1.dpuf

National Endowment for the Arts. (2009–2010). *Artists in a year of recession: Impact on jobs in 2008.* Research Note #97. Washington, DC: National Endowment for the Arts.

National Endowment for the Arts. (2010). *Artist unemployment rates for 2008 and 2009: An addendum to NEA Research Note #97.* Washington, DC: National Endowment for the Arts.

Novick, J., & Novick, K. K. (1996). *Fearful symmetry: The development and treatment of sadomasochism.* Lanham, MD: Jason Aronson/Rowman & Littlefield.

Pavlov, I. P. (1927). *Conditioined reflexes: An investigation of the psysiological activity of the cerebral cortex* (G. V. Anrep, Trans.). London: Oxford University Press.

Salmon, P. G., & Meyer, R. G. (1992). *Notes from the green room.* New York, NY: Lexington Books.

Schafer, R. (1983). *The analytic attitude.* New York, NY: Basic Books.

Shedler, J. (2002). A new language for psychoanalytic diagnosis. *Journal of the American Psychoanalytic Association, 50,* 429–456.

Shedler J. (2010). The efficacy of psychodynamic psychotherapy. *American Psychology, 65*(2), 98–109.

Shedler, J. (2013, October 2). Where is the evidence for evidence-based therapies? *Psychology Today.* Retrieved from http://www.psychologytoday.com/blog/psychologically-minded/201310/where-is-the-evidence-evidence-based-therapies.

Skinner, B. F. (1953). *Science and human behavior.* New York, NY: Macmillan.

Skinner, B. F. (1969). *Contingencies of reinforcement: A theoretical analysis.* New York, NY: Appleton-Century-Crofts.

Spahn, C., Hildenbrandt, H., & Seidenglanz, K. (2001). Effectiveness of a prophylactic course to prevent playing-related health problems of music students. *Medical Problems of Performing Artists, 16*(1), 24–31.

Wachtel, P. L. (2010). Beyond "ESTs": Problematic assumptions in the pursuit of evidence-based practice. *Psychoanalytic Psychology, 27,* 251–272.

Watson, J. B. (1024/1939). *Behaviorism.* New York, NY: Norton.

Weinberger, D. R., & Radulescu, E. (2016). Finding the elusive psychiatric "lesion" with 21st-century neuroanatomy: A note of caution. *American Journal of Psychiatry, 173*(1), 27–33.

Westen, D. (1999). The scientific status of unconscious processes: Is Freud really dead? *Journal of the American Psychoanalytic Association, 47,* 1061–1106.

Yerkes, R. M., & Dodson, J. D. (1908). The relation of strength of stimulus to rapidity of habit-formation. *Journal of Comparative Neurology and Psychology, 18,* 459–482.

INDEX

Note: Tables and figures are indicated by t and f following the page/paragraph number.

mother and, 158
symptoms of, 123
tantrums of, 123
teenagers, 132–34, 159
young, 158
chillout techniques, 22–25
cholesterol, 9
classical conditioning, 100–103,
101n1, 178
cognitions, 16, 20, 35, 81t. *See also*
thoughts
cognitive behavior therapy (CBT),
21n2, 143, 178–79
A B C model and,
108n1, 112–13
definition of, 107–10
psychodynamic theory
and, 110–11
relabeling and revising
responses, 110–13
self-statements and, 109–11
self-talk in, 108–9
in virtual recital, 148–56
cognitive relabeling
(restructuring), 86, 110–13,
157, 162, 179
cold hands, 8, 21, 35, 62, 65,
88, 143–44
collaboration, 132, 165–66
communication, 11–14, 90–91
comparison, 87
competence, 13, 16, 92, 171
competition, 17, 131, 136
conflict and, 45–46, 51
jealousy and, 151
loss and, 47
motivation of, 151
rejection and, 167
symptoms and, 53
teachers and, 52–53, 160
concentration, xxi, 8, 17, 21,
51, 153

conditioning
behavior, teachers and, 103–6
classical, 100–103, 101n1, 178
definition of, 101
operant, 103–5, 180
confidentiality, 147, 166
conflict, 39, 179
childhood and, 45–46
competition and, 45–46, 51
consequences and, 41
desire for approval and, 40
development and, 40, 121
discussing, 50
emotions and, 59
examples of, 41, 46–48
fear and, 40, 51
loss and, 48
motivation and, 40
recognizing, 41–42
self-esteem and, 41
self-reflection and, 53
symptoms and, 40, 50–53
unconscious and, 62
usefulness of, 46
wishes and, 51
conscious, 63, 78, 179
consequences, 26, 41
control, 145
coping, 18, 27, 155
cortisol, 8
countertransference, 71–72, 74, 76,
97–98, 179
creative energy, xxii
curiosity, 66, 130
curriculum, music school,
167–69

death, 47–48, 52
deep breathing, 22–23, 150–51,
152, 153
denial, 79t, 82–83, 89, 179
depression, 88, 137, 141, 167

symptoms, 1–2, 17, 108, 181.
See also body/mind
connection
beta blocking drugs and,
114–16, 150
of children, 123
as clues, 25, 32–35, 38
cognitions and, 35
cold hands, 8, 21, 35, 62, 65,
88, 143–44
competition and, 53
as complaints, 23
conflict and, 40, 50–53
definition of, 16
as disguise, 162
ego defense and, 79, 81t, 88–89
emotions and, 20, 35
experience of, 19
feelings and, 33, 35
identifying, 19–22, 25
magical thinking and, 49–50
origin of, 37, 162–63
physical, 8–9, 15–16, 20, 23,
51–52, 62, 73, 81t, 114–15,
116, 143–44, 150, 152–53, 160
psychological, 20, 23, 51–52, 81t
as signals, 32–35
unconscious and, 62
uniqueness of, 76
as warnings, 33
systematic desensitization, 157

talent, 10
tantrums, 123
teachers
actions for, 28–29
advice of, xix
attitudes of, 71–72
audience and, 13
competition and, 52–53, 160
concepts for virtual
recital, 144–45
conditioning behavior
and, 103–6
countertransference, 71–72,
97–98, 179
development and, 172
emotions of, 52
empathy of, 12, 96
feelings of, 71
implications for, xx, 14, 23,
31, 53–54, 76, 96–98,
105–6, 119, 127–28, 129–30,
132, 134, 136, 137–38, 139,
141–42, 156
learning theories as guidelines
for, 99–100
listening skills of, 42–43
mental health and, 4–6
as new parents, 120–22, 124,
127, 140
openness of, 14
plan for virtual recital, 145
practicing and, 9–10
private life of, 76
professionalism of, 71–72, 74, 76
referrals, 162, 165–67, 169
reputation of, 160
as role models, 132, 159
role of, 171–73
skills of, 99–100
transference and, 66–69,
75, 97–98
tune-ups for, 164–65
teacher-student relationships, xix,
99, 175
communication in, 11–14
emotions and, 4
professionalism, 71–72, 74, 76
shame and, 89–90
transference, 67–68
validation of feelings, 11–14
technique, 20, 42–44, 149–50
teenagers, 80, 132–34, 159